THE GLUTEN-FREE COOKBOOK

THE GLUTEN-FREE COOKBOOK

OVER 50 DELICIOUS AND NUTRITIOUS RECIPES TO SUIT EVERY OCCASION

ANNE SHEASBY

LORENZ BOOKS

First published in 1998 by Lorenz Books
27 West 20th Street, New York, NY 10011

LORENZ BOOKS are available for bulk purchase for sales promotion and for
premium use. For details, write or call the sales director, Lorenz Books,
27 West 20th Street, New York, NY 10011; (800) 354-9657.

© 1998 Anness Publishing Inc.

Lorenz Books is an imprint of
Anness Publishing Inc.

ISBN 1 85967 672 3

Publisher: Joanna Lorenz
Senior Cookbook Editor: Linda Fraser
Designer: Carole Perks
Photography: William Lingwood
Food for Photography: Lucy McKelvie
Styling: Claire Louise Hunt
Illustrator: Madeleine David
Indexer: Hilary Bird
Nutritional Analysis: Helen Daniels

Printed and bound in Singapore

1 3 5 7 9 10 8 6 4 2

CONTENTS

INTRODUCTION

If you've bought this cookbook, the chances are that you, or someone close to you, has been advised to follow a gluten-free diet. The most likely reason for this is a diagnosis of celiac disease, but you may have a wheat allergy or a relatively rare skin condition. Whatever the reason, being faced with following a diet for life may seem rather daunting. The good news is that gluten is not particularly difficult to avoid: a huge range of delicious foods remains open to you, and you won't need to be singled out from family or friends, as everything you eat can be enjoyed by them, too.

WHAT IS GLUTEN?

Gluten is a protein that occurs naturally in wheat and rye and is related to similar proteins in oats and barley. When the grain is milled, it is the gluten that gives the flour its strength and elasticity. Most people ingest gluten without any difficulty, but in genetically susceptible individuals it can cause problems.

CELIAC DISEASE

This lifelong condition, caused by a sensitivity to gluten, affects about one in 1,000 to one in 1,500 people world-wide. Celiac disease was once thought of as a disease exclusive to childhood, but while the condition is present from birth, the symptoms may not appear until much later in life. Nowadays, far more adults than children have the condition; the majority of newly diagnosed celiacs are aged between 30 and 45, with a significant number falling in the over-60s category.

The condition is known to run in families, and some celiacs without obvious symptoms are detected when their relatives are being studied. It is suspected that many cases of celiac disease remain undiagnosed, so the number of cases may in fact be higher.

Celiac disease was first recognized by the Greeks in the second century AD; the word *celiac* is derived from the Greek *koiliakos*, meaning "suffering in the bowels," an apt description of a condition that affects the gastrointestinal tract.

In a person with a healthy digestive system, food that has been broken down in the stomach and duodenum passes through the small intestine, where threadlike projections called

SYMPTOMS

The symptoms of celiac disease vary widely and can be attributable to other medical conditions, so it is vital to seek a proper diagnosis before starting a gluten-free diet.

An adult with celiac disease may be chronically tired (often due to anemia resulting from poor iron and folic acid absorption). Mouth ulcers are common, as is abdominal discomfort, often with a feeling of fullness or bloating. Sufferers can be very ill indeed, with vomiting, diarrhea and severe weight loss. There may be a long history of stomach upsets, or the sufferer may suddenly have developed the condition.

The symptoms of celiac disease may become apparent at any age. In a baby, for instance, the first sign of a problem is usually at about three months, when the child is being weaned. If a child who previously enjoyed his or her feeds becomes miserable at mealtimes, refuses foods and stops gaining weight, medical advice should be sought.

If undiagnosed and untreated, a baby with the celiac condition will lose weight, become listless and irritable and develop a swollen potbelly. The stools will be unusually pale, with an offensive odor, and there may be diarrhea and vomiting. If the condition persists, the child will eventually become seriously ill.

Left: Seek medical advice before you or one of your family embarks on a gluten-free diet.

villi absorb essential nutrients.

When a celiac eats food containing gluten, the intestine responds to the food as if it were a foreign body. There is an immune response: the lining of the intestine becomes inflamed and this causes the villi to become flattened. As a result, the surface area is reduced and the gut is no longer able to absorb nutrients efficiently. Over time, weight loss and wasting can occur, leading to malnutrition.

Precisely how or why gluten is harmful to the small intestine is not known, but the only cure for the diagnosed celiac is to follow a strict gluten-free diet for life. Once gluten is withdrawn from the diet, the flattened villi in the lining of the small intestine will gradually return to normal. Gluten can never be reintroduced, however; once the body has become sensitized to gluten, it will always be affected by it. The occasional minor slipup may only have minimal effect, but if the diet is not followed strictly and even small quantities of foods containing gluten are eaten regularly, the unpleasant symptoms will return, causing discomfort as well as further damage to the delicate intestine.

If you are uncertain as to whether a given food contains gluten, avoid it. It is simply not worth taking the risk.

When an individual embarks upon a gluten-free diet, the results are sometimes dramatic, but more often he or she will see a gradual but continuing improvement. It takes time for the lining of the small intestine to grow again.

Some celiacs find that very fatty foods irritate their stomachs; these are often best avoided, particularly in the early stages of the diet. However, it is important not to lose sight of the fact that everyone suffers from illness at some time and a celiac who feels under the weather may simply have succumbed to a bug that is doing the rounds; before jumping to conclusions, consult a doctor.

WHEAT ALLERGY OR WHEAT INTOLERANCE AND DERMATITIS HERPETIFORMIS

People suffering from an allergy or intolerance to wheat may also benefit from a strict gluten-free diet, as will anyone suffering from the rare skin complaint known as dermatitis herpetiformis.

SYMPTOMS

Wheat allergy or intolerance can cause a wide range of symptoms including aches and pains in the joints and muscles, coughing, sneezing, runny nose, watery and itchy eyes, skin rashes, eczema, faintness and dizziness. The sufferer may have a swollen throat or tongue and find it difficult to swallow. Chest pains, palpitations, nausea, vomiting, diarrhea, tiredness, lethargy, depression and mood swings have also been reported. Of course, these symptoms can be indicative of all sorts of conditions, and sufferers should always seek sound medical advice before assuming that wheat is the culprit.

If their suspicions are confirmed, however, they should exclude all sources of wheat, including wheat protein and wheat starch. Some sufferers may also react to other grains, such as rye, corn and barley, but unlike celiacs, many people who are allergic to wheat can tolerate oats.

A product labeled as being gluten-free may also be wheat-free, but this is not inevitable; there may certainly be no gluten present, but the product may contain wheat starch. Always check the packaging or seek more information.

Dermatitis herpetiformis—also caused by a sensitivity to gluten—is a rare skin condition that causes an extremely itchy skin rash that consists of red raised patches and small blisters, appearing most often on the elbows, buttocks and knees. The first appearance of the skin rash most often occurs in people who are aged between 15 and 40. The condition is rare in children, although the symptoms can appear at any age.

Dermatitis herpetiformis affects about 1 in 20,000 people (slightly more males than females) and must be diagnosed by a specialist in skin diseases.

Because gluten is implicated, people with dermatitis herpetiformis may also have celiac disease, although the symptoms will usually be mild. A permanent gluten-free diet will alleviate both the skin condition and the mild celiac disease, although it may take some time for the rash to disappear entirely.

DIAGNOSIS

Whether the sufferer is an adult or a child, it is vital that the celiac condition is properly diagnosed by a doctor before a gluten-free diet is embarked upon.

Diagnosis is by a standard test—a jejunal biopsy—performed under light sedation in the outpatient department of a hospital. A gastroenterologist will remove a small piece of the villi from the lining of the small intestine. Microscopic examination will reveal whether or not the celiac condition is present.

If the diagnosis is positive, all the patient needs to do to restore the intestine to health is to adhere strictly to a full and varied gluten-free diet. In the short term, the doctor may prescribe a course of vitamins or mineral supplements.

ACHIEVING A HEALTHY DIET

For all of us, whether we are celiacs or not, a healthy, balanced diet is basically one that provides the body with all the nutrients it needs for daily maintenance, growth and repair, plus enough energy for daily requirements. A balanced diet should include protein, carbohydrate, fats and fiber in the correct proportions, plus a good balance of vitamins and minerals. Eating well and wisely promotes good health, boosts energy levels, improves resistance and helps to protect the body against heart disease, bowel disorders, certain cancers and obesity.

Most of our dietary problems have arisen because of changes in lifestyle. It is ironic that in an age where food has never been easier to obtain, the desire for instant gratification and "instant" meals has led to an entire industry producing convenience foods that often contain less fiber, minerals and vitamins than home-cooked alternatives, but more fats and sugars. Such foods are tasty, but do not satisfy our hunger for long, so we fill up on snacks like chips and cookies.

Variety is the key to a healthy diet. To obtain all the nutrients (including vitamins and minerals) that we need, it is recommended that we choose a variety of foods from the five main food groups every day, and serve them in different ways.

We should be eating plenty of fruit and vegetables (at least five portions daily, not including potatoes). Also on the menu should be cereals and pasta (gluten-free if required), rice and potatoes; moderate amounts of lean meat, fish, poultry and dairy products and only small amounts of foods containing fat or sugar.

We all need to eat less fat (especially saturated fat). Ways to do this include cutting off visible fat on meat, broiling rather than frying foods where possible and looking for low-fat and reduced-fat alternatives.

Cutting down on sugar and salt is recommended. It is also important to eat regularly (three meals a day), drink less alcohol and take more exercise.

THE FIVE MAIN FOOD GROUPS

Above: Meat, poultry, fish and vegetarian protein foods—eat in moderation.

Above: Milk and other dairy foods—watch your fat intake.

Above: Foods that contain fat and foods that contain sugar—limit these.

Left: Fruit and vegetables—aim to eat at least five portions of fruit and vegetables (not counting potatoes) every day.

Right: Potatoes, rice, bread, cereals and pasta (gluten-free where needed).

DIETARY FIBER

Some celiacs worry that, because they are unable to eat wheat and wheat bran, they will not be getting enough fiber. Fiber intake for a celiac can be increased by adding soy bran or rice bran to food, eating plenty of plain nuts and fresh fruits and vegetables (with the skins left on) and eating brown rice, beans and pulses. Commercially produced high-fiber, gluten-free foods are available.

Before diagnosis, many celiacs suffer from weight loss and wasting, due to their bodies' inability to absorb the nutrients from food. However, quite the opposite often occurs once

Below: High-fiber foods include, clockwise from left, split peas, green and red lentils, brown rice, pinto beans, red kidney beans and mixed nuts.

a celiac has become established on a gluten-free diet. The person's appetite returns and food becomes more interesting, so there is a temptation to eat more food than the body needs, resulting in weight gain. Excess weight gain can be a problem for both celiacs and non-celiacs alike, and the remedy is the same for both—to follow a sensible diet so that the weight is lost slowly and safely.

When embarking on a gluten-free diet, some celiacs find it is easier to start simply, with plain foods, such as poached salmon with new potatoes and snow peas or grilled lamb chops with roasted peppers, followed by fresh fruit desserts. There'll be time enough for more elaborate dishes later, when the cook has mastered the art of making sauces, pastries and other desserts using gluten-free ingredients.

QUICK AND EASY HIGH-FIBER, GLUTEN-FREE FOODS

All these easy-to-prepare dishes are high in fiber and gluten-free:
- Homemade vegetable, bean or lentil soup.
- A baked potato filled with gluten-free baked beans.
- Corn on the cob.
- A simple salad made from cooked brown rice or buckwheat mixed with diced celery, carrot, tomatoes, yellow pepper, scallions and walnuts.
- Sticks of fresh pineapple rolled in honey and coated in sesame seeds.
- Fruit salad made from bananas, apples, plums and orange segments, with a few chopped dates and raisins.
- Banana freezes—ripe, peeled bananas spread with honey, rolled in crushed roasted hazelnuts, then frozen on baking parchment.

FOODS TO EAT AND FOODS TO AVOID

A gluten-free diet excludes all foods containing any form of wheat, barley, rye and oats. (Some celiacs can tolerate oats with no adverse effects, but many cannot, so it is a wise precaution to exclude them.) Items like bread, cakes, cookies, pasta and pastries made from wheat flour are obvious sources of gluten, but it is also essential to be aware of less obvious sources, as when wheat flour has been used to coat or dust foods or thicken soups, stews, gravies and puddings. Bread crumbs, for instance, are used in stuffings and coatings or as a filler in foods like sausages and hamburgers.

FOODS THAT ARE NATURALLY GLUTEN-FREE

● Fresh or frozen plain meat, fish or poultry, without stuffing or a crumb coating; canned or prepackaged plain cooked meats, such as corned beef or ham (without any coating); smoked and cured pure meats; fresh, frozen or cured plain fish or shellfish; fish canned in oil, brine or water.

Above: Anchovies canned in oil, smoked mackerel and cooked shrimp are all naturally gluten-free.

● Fresh or frozen plain vegetables or fruit, dried fruit and vegetables (including pulses), plain canned fruit in syrup or juice, vegetables canned in brine, water or juice, plain vegetables pickled in vinegar, potato chips.
● Eggs.
● Nuts and seeds of all types, provided they are plain; also peanut butter.
● Gelatin and agar-agar.
● Dairy produce including all plain cheeses (but not spreads or processed cheese), milk, dairy cream, plain yogurt, fromage frais; also plain dried milk, evaporated and condensed milk.
● Fats and oils, including pure vegetable oils, such as olive, sunflower and canola; butter, margarine (as long as it does not contain wheat-germ oil), reduced-fat and low-fat spreads.
● Sugar in all its forms, including pure honey, syrup and molasses.
● Fruit conserves, jam and marmalade.
● Flavorings, seasonings, herbs and spices, including salt, freshly ground black pepper, black peppercorns, cider vinegar and wine vinegar, pure whole or ground spices, tomato paste and garlic purée, pure food flavorings, such as vanilla and almond extracts, pure food colorings.
● Breakfast cereals, such as rice crispies, puffed rice, some cornflakes.

Above: Add flavor and color to your meals using black peppercorns, tomato paste, red wine vinegar, pure ground cinnamon, pure food flavorings and colorings.

● Grains, whether whole or ground, including buckwheat flakes and flour, carob flour, cornstarch, gram flour (from ground chickpeas), corn flour, millet flour, potato flour, sorghum flour, soy flour, sweet chestnut flour, teff flour, yam flour, yellow split pea flour, arrowroot, rice (all types, including wild rice; also ground rice and rice flour), hominy grits, millet (also millet flakes and seeds), polenta, quinoa grains, sago and tapioca.
● Good-quality semisweet chocolate.
● Yeast (and yeast extract).
● Pure rice noodles, pure corn, rice and millet pasta, pure buckwheat pasta—check that pastas do not contain added wheat flour, starch or binders.
● Drinks, such as tea, coffee, fruit-flavored sodas, pure fruit juices (preferably unsweetened); also cider, wine, sherry, brandy, port.

Above: Breakfast need not be a problem for celiacs. Eggs, jam or marmalade, milk and rice- and corn-based cereals, such as rice crispies and some cornflakes, are all gluten-free. Serve them with gluten-free toast.

MANUFACTURED FOODS THAT ARE GLUTEN-FREE

A wide range of specially manufactured gluten-free foods is also available. The list includes breads, cakes, cookies, crackers and crispbreads, plus flours, flour mixes, bread and cake mixes, muesli, pastas and rusks. Talk to your doctor, as in certain countries, such as the UK, you may be able to obtain some of these products by prescription. Others can be purchased from druggists or health food stores, or by mail order, although they can be costly.

Manufactured foods that have been specifically made for the market by reputable companies are very useful. They look like the wheat-flour products they are intended to replace, so will go unremarked at occasions like children's parties.

Many everyday canned and packaged foods are also gluten-free.

When using products such as gluten-free flours or bread or cake mixes for the first time, always follow the manufacturer's guidance and instructions on usage.

FOODS TO AVOID

The following foods always contain flour made from wheat, barley, rye or oats, so must be avoided:

● Wheat berries or grains; wheat bran; wheat flakes; wheat flour, such as all-purpose or white bread flour, brown, granary and whole-wheat flours; wheat meal; wheat protein; wheat starch; bulgur; couscous; cracked wheat, durum wheat (used in pasta); kibbled wheat; rusks; semolina; wheat germ.
● Pearl barley, pot barley, barley flakes, barley flour, barley meal.
● Rye flakes, rye flour, rye meal.
● Oats, oat flakes, jumbo oats, rolled oats, oatmeal, oat bran, oat germ.
● Spelt (flour and American pasta made from a grain related to wheat), kamut (in Italian whole-grain pasta).
● Triticale (wheat/rye hybrid grain).

COMMON FOODS THAT MAY CONTAIN GLUTEN

● Dry goods like baking powder, malt, curry powder, mustard powder, MSG (monosodium glutamate flavor enhancer), gravy mixes, spices and spice mixes, pepper compounds and ready-ground white pepper, bouillon cubes.
● Pasta (durum wheat pastas are out, and some Asian noodles, though made from other grains, contain wheat).
● Some cornflakes.
● Salad dressings, soy sauce, malt vinegar.
● Some processed cheese spreads, some flavored yogurts.
● Sausages (and sausage rolls), meat pies, beefburgers, pâtés, foods coated in batter or bread crumbs.
● Dry roasted nuts.
● Communion wafers (gluten-free wafers are available by mail order).
● Beers, malted milk drinks.

Above right: Some common foods, such as malt vinegar, pasta made with wheat, dry-roasted nuts, mustards and malted milk drinks, contain gluten and must be avoided.

Below: The range of specially manufactured gluten-free foods includes cookies, cereal, corn pasta and gluten-free flours.

FOOD LABELING

By law, all manufacturers have to mark or label food with a list of ingredients. Sources of gluten are not always obvious, however. If you read any of the following words on a food label, alarm bells should ring and you should ask for more information: binder, binding, cereal, cereal protein, corn, cornstarch, edible starch, flour, food starch, modified starch, rusk, special edible starch, starch, thickener, thickening or vegetable protein.

GLUTEN-FREE COOKING

There is nothing special about gluten-free cooking other than the fact that some ingredients are replaced with alternatives that are equally varied and interesting. Once you familiarize yourself with the list of foods that can safely be served (and note the no-no's), it is simply a matter of making delicious dishes that everyone can enjoy. You will rapidly get into the habit of using a variety of alternative starches for baking, cooking, thickening, binding and coating, and in doing so will discover just how delicious many of the less familiar grains can be.

If you are new to gluten-free cooking, you will probably prefer to start with simple no-risk dishes like grilled dishes with fresh vegetables. This will have obvious health advantages, but don't abandon the treats. If you continue to serve pies and cakes, make them gluten-free, so everyone in the family will be able to enjoy their favorite foods—and the celiac won't feel isolated.

USING GLUTEN-FREE FLOURS

Because gluten is the protein that strengthens and binds dough in baking, you may need to find alternative binding agents when using gluten-free flours. Follow recipes for baked goods closely, as they will have been specially formulated to allow for this potential problem. A combination of starches often works better than a single type, and adding egg, pectin powder, grated apple or mashed banana may help to bind gluten-free dough.

BINDING BURGERS AND SAUSAGES

Although burgers and sausages are conventionally bound with bread crumbs, they work equally well without. The best hamburgers are made purely from ground beef, and fresh sausage meat will hold together without additional ingredients. If you must use a binder, add rice flour and egg.

AVOIDING WHEAT CONTAMINATION

If you are baking a batch of breads, cakes and pastries (only some of which are gluten-free), be careful to keep ingredients separate so that there is no risk of wheat flour contaminating the gluten-free foods. Wash all utensils thoroughly after each use. For a highly allergic person, it may be sensible to use separate baking pans and cooking utensils. Alternatively—and this is simpler and safer—use gluten-free ingredients for all your cooking.

QUICK TIPS ON GLUTEN-FREE COOKING

● Do not use bread crumbs (unless they are gluten-free) for coating foods. Crushed gluten-free corn-flakes make a good alternative for coating foods and for gratins.

● Do not dust or coat foods with wheat flour prior to cooking—either avoid dusting foods altogether or use naturally gluten-free flours like cornmeal or rice flour.

● Potato flour is useful for thickening gravies, stews, casseroles, sauces and soups.

● Roll gluten-free pastry out on waxed paper, as this makes it easier to lift and to line the pan.

● If gluten-free pastry is very crumbly, press it over the bottom and up the sides of the pan (as when making shortbread) rather than trying to roll it out.

● Grease baking pans before use, even if they are nonstick, or line the pans with baking parchment to prevent sticking.

● It is a good idea to bake a batch of gluten-free breads, cakes and cookies and pop some of them into the freezer. Gluten-free baked goods freeze well and will keep fresh for many weeks. Freeze in portions, so that you can thaw exactly what you need for a packed lunch or afternoon snack.

PANTRY ESSENTIALS

Pack your pantry with these items and you'll always have the makings of a gluten-free meal:

- Gluten-free cornflakes, rice crispies, puffed rice cereal.
- Fish, such as anchovies, sardines or tuna, canned in oil, brine or water.
- Canned cooked meat, such as ham or gluten-free corned beef.
- Vegetables canned in water, brine or juice, pickled vegetables.
- Dried vegetables and beans, plain potato chips.
- Canned fruit in syrup or juice.
- Plain dried fruit, candied cherries.
- Fruit juices and sodas.
- Rice; also rice noodles and other gluten-free pastas.
- Plain nuts (not dry-roasted) and seeds, pure peanut butter.
- Sugars, pure syrups, pure honey, jam, marmalade.
- Dried plain milk, evaporated and condensed milk, tea, pure coffee, good-quality chocolate.

- Naturally gluten-free flours, including rice flour, gluten-free cornstarch, corn flour, cornmeal, potato flour and soy flour; also yeast.
- Ground rice, tapioca, buckwheat flakes, millet flakes, rice flakes.
- Gelatin or agar-agar.
- Pure vegetable oils, wine vinegar or cider vinegar.
- Salt, black peppercorns, dried herbs, pure spices.
- Pure food flavorings and colorings.
- Tomato paste, garlic purée, gluten-free soy sauce.

Above: Essential items for your pantry should include: rice cakes, polenta, pure spices, dried herbs, gluten-free cornstarch, rice noodles, rice and gluten-free flour.

Left: Stock up on naturally gluten-free foods, such as jams and marmalades, canned fruits and vegetables, pickled onions, potato chips, dried fruit and gluten-free breakfast cereals.

GLUTEN-FREE ACCOMPANIMENTS

Potatoes and rice are particularly good sources of natural, gluten-free carbohydrate. They make ideal accompaniments to many dishes and can be served in a wide variety of ways. Explore the potential of gluten-free pastas, too. Rice noodles and corn pasta are delicious, and polenta is marvelous with sauced dishes; try it freshly cooked or cooled, cut into wedges and shallow-fried.

POTATOES

There are few vegetables as versatile as the potato. Tiny new potatoes are delicious boiled or steamed, baked potatoes make a meal in themselves with a tasty topping, and homemade French fries are one treat a gluten-free diet doesn't deny you. Patties, pancakes or croquettes, rolled in crushed gluten-free cornflakes or bread crumbs, make an excellent accompaniment, and mashed potatoes can be served in numerous ways. Always use the right variety of potato for the job. Scrub potatoes and leave the skins on when roasting or making fries for extra texture, flavor and fiber. For a tasty change, try either sweet potatoes or yams.

RICE

There are many different varieties of rice including brown and white, long-grain, short-grain, basmati and risotto rice (arborio), all of which are gluten-free, as is wild rice. Boiled rice can be served as it is, stir-fried or used as the basis for a salad.

Below: Don't just opt for plain boiled long-grain rice; try cooking wild rice, brown rice or arborio rice, for a change.

Above: Potatoes, sweet potatoes and yams are all naturally gluten-free.

RICE NOODLES

These are made from ground rice and water and range in thickness from very thin to wide ribbons and sheets. They are available fresh or dried and are often soaked in warm water before being briefly cooked.

CORN PASTA

Pure corn pasta—made from corn without added binders or starch—is ideal for a gluten-free diet. It comes in a variety of flavors (including parsley, spinach and chile) and in shapes that range from spaghetti to twists and shells. All versions look pretty on the plate and have a good flavor. Corn pasta makes an excellent alternative to durum wheat pasta.

Above: Corn pasta, rice noodles and polenta make marvelous accompaniments.

POLENTA

Coarsely ground cornmeal is a staple food in Italy, where it is often served as an accompaniment instead of rice or pasta. The partly cooked ground grain is whisked into boiling water or stock.

HOW TO COOK POLENTA

Bring 5 cups salted water or stock to a boil in a large saucepan. Sprinkle generous 1 cup polenta into the boiling water, stirring constantly. Cook, uncovered, over very low heat for about 40 minutes, stirring frequently, until cooked and thick. Season and add flavorings, such as cheese, butter, garlic and herbs. Serve hot.

HOW TO COOK BROWN RICE

Bring 5⅔ cups lightly salted water to a boil in a large saucepan. Add 1¼ cups brown rice. Bring back to a boil, then lower the heat and simmer, uncovered, for 25–35 minutes, until the rice is tender but retains a bit of bite. Drain the rice in a sieve, rinse with boiling water, then drain thoroughly again.

HOW TO COOK RICE NOODLES

Bring 2 quarts lightly salted water to a boil in a large saucepan. Turn off the heat and add 2¼ cups rice noodles. Stir the noodles with a fork to separate them, cover and set aside for 4 minutes. Drain and serve. If serving the noodles cold, rinse in cold water and drain again.

GLUTEN-FREE SNACKS AND FINGER FOODS

We all enjoy snacks sometimes, particularly when the munchies strike. When baking, make extra gluten-free cakes and cookies and freeze the surplus in slices. That way, you can thaw individual portions as needed. Occasional treats, such as a bar of gluten-free chocolate or a package of plain potato chips, won't do any harm, but it is useful to have a good selection of healthy and delicious gluten-free snacks and treats available, ready to keep hunger pangs at bay.
- Fresh fruit, such as apples, pears, mangoes, kiwifruit, pineapple wedges, peaches, apricots and oranges.
- Dried fruit, such as apricots, peaches, pears, apples, prunes or mixed dried fruit.
- Gluten-free crackers, crispbreads and rice cakes. Serve them with plain cheese, such as Cheddar, Red Leicester, Stilton or Emmental.
- Wedges of gluten-free fruit cake.

- Plain nuts, such as walnuts, almonds or hazelnuts or a mixture of nuts and dried fruit, mixed seeds or a mixture of mixed seeds and plain nuts.
- Plain yogurt to which you can add chopped fresh fruit for a sweet treat, or finely diced cucumber and a trace of

Above: Healthy gluten-free snacks include nuts, mixed nuts and raisins, cheese and rice crackers, and raw vegetable crudités.

crushed garlic for a savory surprise; also plain or flavored fromage frais and gluten-free fruit yogurts.

CHILDREN AND CELIAC DISEASE

Children diagnosed as having celiac disease can be treated exactly like their peers in all ways but one: they will have to avoid foods containing gluten for the rest of their lives. But as we have already seen, this is not particularly difficult and will have positive results in terms of health.

If parents treat the situation in a calm, matter-of-fact way, explaining to the child why there are some foods that he or she cannot eat, but not making such an issue of it that the child feels either anxious or isolated, then their son or daughter will rapidly come to terms with the celiac condition, will adapt to the diet (especially if what's on the menu looks and tastes virtually the same as whatever other children are eating) and will be able to enjoy life to the full.

It is a good idea to avoid giving any child foods containing gluten until he is at least six months old. The child with celiac disease will thrive during this time. Only when gluten is introduced into the diet—probably as oatmeal or baby rusks—will the celiac child develop problems. If this should happen, it is important to see your doctor without delay. Don't change the child's diet in the meantime, as this might make the condition more difficult to diagnose.

On diagnosis, you will doubtless be given advice about what to feed your baby. Mashed banana or cooked apple, vegetable purée, puréed steamed fish or chicken, plain yogurt—these are standard baby foods—and when you make them yourself you can control the ingredients absolutely.

As your baby grows, you can begin introducing him or her to a wide range of gluten-free foods.

Family, friends and anyone who cares for the child should be told about the celiac condition (preferably not in front of the child) so that they will not inadvertently offer foods that contain gluten.

It is easier for the celiac child—and simpler in terms of cooking—if all members of the immediate family eat the same gluten-free foods at mealtimes. When your son or daughter starts play group or nursery school, explain to the organizer about the celiac condition and pack gluten-free snacks for playtime. Molding play dough is a favorite pastime for young children, and parents should be aware that this product does contain wheat flour—just in case the child decides to put it in his mouth, as many young children do.

SCHOOL DAYS

When your child starts school, it is wise to let the staff know about the condition and explain what it entails. In the case of school lunches, it is advisable to consult with the teacher or school cook: some school lunches will be naturally gluten-free, and the child who chooses sensibly (under supervision) will be able to enjoy a school

Left: Playing with play dough is a favorite pastime for young children, but be aware that this product contains wheat flour.

Above: When your child starts school, make sure that their teacher is aware of the child's condition and what it entails

lunch with his friends. Alternatively, your son or daughter could take a gluten-free packed lunch. Most primary schools set aside a special area so that children who have brought their own food can eat together, so this can be just as sociable—just make sure your child knows not to swap!

Invitations to other children's parties won't pose problems if you call the hosts beforehand and explain the situation. It is easiest if the celiac child takes his or her own gluten-free food; try to find out what is likely to be on the menu, so that you can send along something that is broadly similar. The child will soon get used to taking his or her own food to parties, and will learn which familar foods are gluten-free and thus okay to eat.

If the party is your own, simply serve gluten-free food for everyone. This is by no means second best: as the recipes in this book prove, gluten-free food can be every bit as delicious as the alternatives.

There is bound to be a time when your child accidentally eats something containing gluten. Don't panic—these mishaps will cause minor upsets, but as long as the child continues on a gluten-free diet, the symptoms will pass in a few days.

If your child is ill, it is equally important not to assume automatically that he or she has eaten something containing gluten; celiac children succumb to tummy bugs, just like everyone else.

As celiac children get older, particularly in their teenage years, they like to be one of the crowd and don't wish to be seen as different or an outsider. This is an important time for parents to be supportive and encourage the child to continue following a gluten-free diet.

CHILDREN'S PACKED LUNCHES

- Gluten-free mini scones, muffins or meringues.
- Small packages or bags of dried fruit, such as raisins, dried apricots, mango, pears, peaches or apples, or mixed dried fruit or prunes.
- Gluten-free snacks, such as plain potato chips and plain mixed nuts or nuts and raisins (avoid dry-roasted nuts, which may contain gluten).
- Raw carrot or cucumber sticks.
- Rice salad, gluten-free pasta salad, tuna and bean salad, potato salad, other home-made mixed salads.
- Homemade gluten-free soups.
- Cold potatoes with or without a gluten-free dressing.
- Hard-boiled eggs.
- Fresh fruit, such as apples, pears, bananas, oranges, satsumas, clementines, kiwifruit, cherries, grapes.
- Fresh fruit salad.
- Plain or fruit-flavored fromage frais, plain yogurts (to which you can add your own choice of chopped fresh fruits) or pure fruit-flavored yogurts.
- Drinks suitable for packed lunches include fruit drinks, diluted unsweetened fruit juices, milk, homemade milk shakes and water.

Below: Fresh and dried fruits, nuts, yogurt, carrot sticks and potato chips are easy to pack into a lunch box. If the school doesn't provide a drink, then include a carton of fresh fruit juice or a small bottle of mineral water, too.

COOKING FOR A CELIAC CHILD

Make the menu as varied as possible and be sure to include typical favorites like pizzas (gluten-free), hamburgers and sausages. Bought burgers and sausages often contain bread crumbs, so make your own gluten-free alternatives.

Packed lunches should be as colorful and as interesting as you can make them. Sandwiches made from gluten-free breads are always popular. Try Rice, Buckwheat and Corn Bread or Cheese and Onion Corn Bread, add your child's favorite gluten-free filling and you have the perfect finger food. For more packed lunch suggestions, see the list above. If you include salads or desserts, use small containers with good seals and remember to pack a fork or spoon. A small thermos is ideal for transporting hot soup or a cold drink.

Don't forget the treats: meringues may not do your child's teeth much good, but they'll do wonders for his or her morale.

ENTERTAINING

Sharing food with friends is one of life's great pleasures, whether this consists of a family gathering, a casual supper or a sophisticated dinner party. What we serve depends on the occasion and the appetites and tastes of our guests, but the menu should be planned with an eye to color, complementary flavors and contrasting textures. It is important to be aware of any special dietary needs —not just those of the celiac in the family—so that these can be accommodated in such a way that nobody feels singled out. Serving gluten-free food to everyone is the easiest option. This will not pose any particular problems, as the range of healthy, nutritious dishes available is so varied and interesting, and it will be easy to incorporate choices for vegetarian or diabetic guests. On the next few pages you will find menu suggestions for all kinds of occasions.

GLUTEN-FREE FOOD FOR GROWN-UP GUESTS

Cooking for adults implies a certain sophistication, although this is not necessarily the case, as anyone who has catered to the man or woman who always insists on meat and potatoes will appreciate. As a rule, however, grown-ups will eagerly try something new and exciting. They will enjoy sampling rolls, pancakes or pastries made from unfamiliar grains and will be eager to taste your homemade ice cream. Many of your favorite dishes will be naturally gluten-free, and others can easily be adapted.

Note: Where specific dishes are listed, the recipes can be found in the recipe section of the book.

MENU 1

Prosciutto and Olive Bruschetta
Warm Chicken Salad with
Hazelnut Dressing
or Spicy Carrot Soup with
Croutons
Baked Trout with Wild
Mushrooms with sautéed
potatoes, steamed green beans,
braised carrots
or Pancetta and Fava Bean
Risotto with mixed green salad
Rich Chocolate Mousse with
Glazed Kumquats
Summer Strawberry Roulade
Selection of red and white wines,
mineral water

MENU 2

Vegetable crudités and plain chips
with dips, such as yogurt and
chive, garlic and chile tomato,
curried gluten-free mayonnaise
Grilled Vegetable Pizza
Tuna, Zucchini and
Pepper Frittata
Wild Mushroom and
Broccoli Tart
Thai Chicken and
Vegetable Curry
Lemon Cheesecake with
Wild Berries
Chocolate Meringues with Mixed
Fruit Compote
Selection of beers, wines, water

CHOICES FOR CHILDREN'S BIRTHDAY PARTIES

Children love birthday parties. No matter how appealing the package offered by the local pizza parlor or fast-food restaurant, most children would just as soon celebrate at home with presents, party games and a colorful spread with plenty of choice. When giving a party for your celiac child, avoid complications by making sure that all the food is gluten-free. You don't need to provide a vast amount—most children pick, mix and nibble—but it is important that the eats include plenty of any sweet and savory treats currently popular on the peer-group party circuit.

MENU 3

Mini chicken satés
Cheese cubes and pineapple
chunks on toothpicks
Grilled bacon and banana rolls
Baked potato skins with a variety
of homemade dips, such as herb
or garlic soured cream, home-
made Thousand Island, fresh
tomato salsa
Chocolate Chip Cookies
Chocolate-dipped strawberries
and grapes
Strawberry yogurt fool
Home-made gluten-free novelty
birthday cake
Fruit juice, water, fruit sodas

MENU 4

Party sandwiches made using
gluten-free bread with a variety of
gluten-free fillings, such as tuna
and gluten-free mayonnaise, egg
salad, ham and tomato, cheese
and cucumber
Spiced chicken drumsticks
Plain potato chips
Golden Raisin and Cinnamon
Chewy Bars
Chocolate rice crispie cakes
Homemade ice cream
Mini fruit kebabs
Homemade gluten-free novelty
birthday cake
Homemade thick fruit milk shakes

FAMILY MEALS

Cooking for the family can be satisfying and fun, but it can easily turn into a boring chore. The very fact that you have to do it every day makes it easy to slip into the habit of serving the same old thing week in and week out. When you are catering for a celiac, there's a particular danger of sticking to a few tried and tested gluten-free dishes. You probably promise yourself that you'll extend your recipe repertoire one day—but you never seem to have the time. That's why we've listed some simple suggestions for gluten-free main courses and desserts, with minimum preparation and maximum family appeal. Use them in addition to the full-scale recipes that follow.

QUICK AND EASY GLUTEN-FREE MAIN COURSES

- Cook corn pasta, toss with olive oil and add a sprinkling of Parmesan cheese shavings.
- Charbroil chicken breasts and serve with a tomato and basil salsa (*right*).
- Panfry thick cod or salmon steaks in butter and olive oil; add plenty of chopped herbs and a squeeze of lime juice just before serving with roasted Mediterranean vegetables.
- Skewer lean lamb, chunks of bell pepper and thin wedges of red onion on kebab sticks, baste with olive oil and ground cumin and broil or grill until cooked and golden brown.
- Cook polenta, spoon it around the outside of a serving platter and fill the center with ratatouille. Offer freshly grated Parmesan separately.
- Marinate strips of pork fillet in a mixture of gluten-free soy sauce, brown sugar and dry sherry. Stir-fry with snow peas, mushrooms, scallions, carrot and celery. Serve over rice noodles.

INSTANT IDEAS FOR GLUTEN-FREE DESSERTS

- Fill a meringue basket with fresh raspberries and top with a spoonful of Mediterranean-style yogurt.
- Panfry canned or fresh pineapple slices in a little butter (add a scant sprinkling of brown sugar if you like) and serve with scoops of homemade vanilla ice cream.
- Serve fresh fruits with a dollop of crème fraîche (*left*).
- Make parfaits by layering fresh prepared summer fruits and slices of banana in tall glasses. Drizzle a little orange liqueur over adult portions. Top with dairy cream or crème fraîche.
- Spear fruit, such as melon balls, strawberries, chunks of kiwifruit and seedless grapes, on small wooden skewers. Serve with a dip made from yogurt and honey.
- Cook a mixture of prunes, dried apricots or pears and raisins in a light syrup. Set aside until quite cool, then add blanched almonds and shelled pistachios. Serve with crème fraîche or dairy cream.
- Fill the center of cored baking apples with chopped dates or mixed dried fruit. Microwave or bake until tender, then drizzle with pure maple syrup and serve alone or with half-and-half.

EATING OUT

Some celiacs are wary of accepting dinner-party invitations, even though they manage their own diet perfectly well at home. They are not alone in this; anyone on a restricted diet is likely to have similar reservations. The simple solution is to call your host, tell him or her about your condition and explain what you are able to eat. Given due warning, most people will be happy to work out a suitable menu and may even relish the challenge.

When eating out in a restaurant, ask the chef if any dishes are gluten-free, or call ahead to check that they can cater for a celiac. To be on the safe side, always choose foods that you know to be completely gluten-free.

DISHES TO CHOOSE

APPETIZERS: Melon, grapefruit, fruit cocktail, melon with prosciutto.

MAIN COURSES: Plain broiled or roast meat or fish served without stuffing, sauce or gravy; plain shellfish or seafood; plain meat and vegetable kebabs; plain cold meat or cheese platters; rice dishes, such as risotto or kedgeree; plain or soufflé omelets.

ACCOMPANIMENTS: Salads without dressings, new potatoes or baked potatoes with gluten-free toppings, rice, plain cooked vegetables.

DESSERTS: Plain fresh fruit or fruit salad served with plain yogurt or dairy cream, meringues or fresh fruit pavlova, plain broiled, poached or stewed fruit, plain cheeses with fruit.

When eating out, foods, such as chicken Kiev (above right), which are coated in bread crumbs, must be avoided, while melon served with prosciutto (below) makes a safe—and delicious—choice for an appetizer.

DISHES TO AVOID

APPETIZERS: Soups, pâtés, terrines, savory mousses, any dish served with a dressing, such as mayonnaise or a thickened sauce or gravy.

MAIN COURSES: Meat, poultry or fish served with a crumb, batter or oatmeal coating or which may have been coated in flour before being fried; sausages; meat patties; roast meat with stuffing or gravy; stews or casseroles; pies; pizzas, curries; pasta dishes.

DESSERTS: Pancakes or crêpes; custards, ice cream and ice cream wafers; baked puddings, such as sponge pudding; cheesecakes; pies and tarts; petits fours; confectionery.

DRINKS TO AVOID: Beer, lager, ale and stout; tomato juice (may contain gluten); chocolate milk (primarily from vending machines); malted drinks; malted chocolate milk; malted milk drinks.

DRINKS TO CHOOSE: Wine, champagne, cider, spirits, such as sherry, whisky and brandy, fruit sodas, fruit juices, tea, pure coffee (not instant). Soft drinks and most sparkling drinks are gluten-free, but avoid any that are cloudy, as these may contain starch.

Below: To accompany your meal, choose alcoholic drinks, such as red and white wine and champagne or spirit-based drinks, such as gin and tonic, or stick to clear sparkling drinks, fresh fruit juice—or water.

SAFE SEASONING

In restaurants and cafeterias, avoid seasoning food with ground white pepper—many caterers "stretch" the pepper by adding wheat flour. To be safe, ask for the pepper mill and grind black pepper directly onto your food.

PICNICS

Picnics provide the perfect opportunity for families and friends to get together. Whether you pack a simple selection of gluten-free sandwiches and snacks, or go all out with an impressive assortment of sweet and savory dishes, there's something special about eating al fresco.

Picnic foods should be fairly easy to carry, quick to serve and easy to eat. Many dishes can be prepared up to a day in advance and kept chilled until ready to transport.

For a simple picnic, serve a selection of plain cold meats and cheeses, with rice bread or a similar gluten-free loaf. Celery sticks, cherry tomatoes and a simple green salad complete the spread, with a gluten-free vinaigrette dressing in a tightly sealed plastic container. Fresh fruit makes the perfect finale.

For a slightly more extravagant picnic, add some dishes from the column on the right. The picnic basket might also contain a selection of salads with suitable dressings (tomato salad with basil and mozzarella; new potatoes with gluten-free herb vinaigrette; green bean salad with almonds) and some gluten-free pâtés. If you pack pickles and chutneys, make sure they are homemade, as some commercial products contain gluten. A big bowl of strawberries or raspberries will make a delicious dessert with tiny meringues and a bowl of dairy cream. Pack plenty of drinks—and don't forget paper napkins, moist towelettes and garbage bags for the disposal of any trash.

Below: Family picnic foods need to be simple and fairy easy to carry—fresh fruit makes the perfect, gluten-free finale.

GLUTEN-FREE PICNIC FOODS

Where specific dishes are listed, the recipes can be found in the recipe section of the book.

● Spiced chicken drumsticks or chicken wings.

● Gluten-free pizza, such as Grilled Vegetable Pizza.

● Crudités, such as carrot and cucumber sticks; cauliflower and broccoli florets; lettuce hearts; zucchini, pepper and fennel sticks; cherry tomatoes; radishes and celery sticks, served with a gluten-free dip, such as plain yogurt mixed with finely diced cucumber, chopped fresh mint or parsley and crushed garlic.

● Wild Mushroom and Broccoli Tart or a similar gluten-free quiche or savory tart.

● Savory Nut Loaf.

● Various salads, including Mixed Leaf and Herb Salad, Rice Salad, Gluten-free Pasta Salad, Potato Salad, Three Bean Salad, Fruit and Nut Coleslaw.

● Gluten-free breads: Rice, Buckwheat and Corn Bread, Cheese and Onion Corn Bread.

● Desserts, such as fresh fruit salad or Summer Fruit Roulade.

● Apple and Orange Muffins, Cinnamon Chewy Bars, Chocolate Chip Cookies, Cherry Coconut Munchies.

● Sponge Layer Cake, Fruit, Nut and Seed Loaf, Gingerbread, Country Apple Cake.

BASIC RECIPES

There is a wide range of stock products on the market including cubes of various flavors, stock powders or granules and fresh chilled stock, but some of these contain gluten, so it is worthwhile making your own gluten-free stocks at home. Homemade stocks add delicious flavor to many different dishes, and they really are simple to make. It is a good idea to prepare one or two batches and freeze them in useful quantities for future use. Cool homemade stocks quickly, pour them into suitable containers (leaving space for expansion) and freeze them for up to 3 months.

CHICKEN STOCK
Makes about 3 cups
1 meaty chicken carcass
6 shallots or 1 onion
1 carrot
2 celery ribs
1 bay leaf
salt and ground black pepper

1 Break or chop the chicken carcass into pieces and place in a large saucepan with 7½ cups cold water.

2 Peel and slice the shallots or onion and carrot, then chop the celery. Add the vegetables to the saucepan with the bay leaf. Stir to mix.

3 Bring to a boil, then partially cover and simmer for 2 hours, skimming off any scum and fat that rises to the surface during cooking.

4 Strain the stock through a sieve, then set aside to cool.

5 When cold, remove and discard all the fat and use the stock or freeze. Once cool, cover and store in the refrigerator for up to 3 days. Season with salt and pepper, as required.

BEEF STOCK
Makes about 3 cups
1 pound beef shank on the bone
1 pound beef or veal bones
1 onion
1 carrot
1 turnip
2 celery ribs
1 leek
1 bouquet garni
salt and ground black pepper

1 Preheat the oven to 425°F. Place the meat and bones in a roasting pan and brown in the oven for about 30 minutes, then place in a large pan with 7½ cups cold water.

2 Peel and slice the onion and carrot, then peel and dice the turnip and chop the celery and leek. Add the vegetables to the saucepan with the bouquet garni. Stir to mix.

3 Bring to a boil, then partially cover and simmer for 2 hours, skimming off any scum and fat that rises to the surface during cooking. Strain the stock through a fine sieve, then set aside to cool. Store as for chicken stock.

VEGETABLE STOCK
Makes about 6¼ cups
1 large onion, sliced
2 carrots, sliced
1 leek, sliced
3 celery ribs, chopped
1 small turnip, diced
1 small parsnip, sliced
1 bouquet garni
salt and ground black pepper

1 Place all the prepared vegetables in a large saucepan with the bouquet garni. Add 7½ cups cold water and stir to mix.

2 Bring to a boil, then partially cover and simmer for about 1 hour, skimming off any scum.

3 Strain the stock through a sieve; use immediately or set aside to cool. Store in the refrigerator for up to 3 days. Alternatively, freeze the stock. Season with salt and pepper, as required.

COOK'S TIP
If you have any vegetable trimmings, such as tomato or onion skins, celery tops or cabbage leaves, add them to the water with the vegetables when making the stock.

GLUTEN-FREE WHITE SAUCE
Makes about 1¼ cups
2 tablespoons gluten-free cornstarch
1¼ cups low-fat milk
1 tablespoon sunflower
 margarine
salt and ground black pepper

1 Place the cornstarch in a bowl and blend with ¼ cup of the milk to make a smooth paste.

2 Heat the remaining milk in a saucepan over medium heat until boiling, then pour onto the blended mixture, whisking constantly to prevent lumps from forming.

3 Return the mixture to the saucepan and bring slowly to a boil, stirring constantly, until the sauce thickens. Lower the heat and simmer gently for 2–3 minutes, then stir in the margarine until melted. Season to taste and serve.

VARIATIONS
To make a thinner, pouring sauce, reduce the quantity of cornstarch to 4–5 teaspoons.
   Replace half the milk with flavorful vegetable or chicken stock or use a half-and-half mixture of stock and white wine in place of the milk.
   Add gluten-free flavorings, such as grated cheese, chopped mixed fresh herbs, lightly sautéed onions, tomato paste, or chopped or sliced cooked wild or button mushrooms, to the sauce for extra flavor.

FRENCH DRESSING
Makes about ⅔ cup
6 tablespoons olive or sunflower oil
2 tablespoons white wine vinegar or
 lemon juice
1 teaspoon Dijon mustard
¼ teaspoon sugar
1 tablespoon chopped fresh mixed
 herbs
salt and ground black pepper

1 Place all the ingredients in a small bowl and whisk together until thoroughly mixed. Alternatively, place all the ingredients in a clean screw-top jar, seal and shake well until thoroughly mixed.

2 Adjust the seasoning and serve immediately or keep in a screw-top jar in the refrigerator for up to 1 week. Shake well before serving.

VARIATION
Crush a small garlic clove and add to the dressing, if desired.

MAYONNAISE
Makes about 1 cup
2 egg yolks
1 teaspoon Dijon mustard
1 tablespoon lemon juice
½ teaspoon salt
ground black pepper
about ⅔ cup olive or sunflower oil

1 Place the egg yolks, mustard, lemon juice, salt, pepper and 1 tablespoon oil in a small blender or food processor. Blend for 30 seconds.

2 With the motor running, gradually add the remaining oil, pouring it through the funnel in a slow, continuous stream, until the mayonnaise is thick, creamy and smooth.

3 Adjust the seasoning, then use immediately or cover and chill. Store for up to 3 days in a covered container in the refrigerator.

VARIATIONS
Add finely chopped garlic, capers, gherkins or cucumber, crumbled blue cheese or chopped fresh mixed herbs.

SOUPS, SNACKS AND SALADS

If you enjoy a steaming bowl of hot soup served with homemade gluten-free bread, or a quick light salad or tasty snack for lunch or supper, you will find a tempting selection of recipes in this chapter. Try, for example, Spicy Carrot Soup with Garlic Croutons, Grilled Vegetable Pizza, Bacon and Herb Rösti or Warm Chicken Salad with Hazelnut Dressing.

Spicy Carrot Soup with Garlic Croutons

INGREDIENTS

Serves 6
1 tablespoon olive oil
1 large onion, chopped
1½ pounds carrots, sliced
1 teaspoon each ground coriander,
    ground cumin and hot chile powder
3¾ cups vegetable or chicken stock
salt and ground black pepper
cilantro sprigs, to garnish

For the garlic croutons
a little olive oil, for frying
2 garlic cloves, crushed
4 slices of gluten-free bread, crusts
    removed, cut into ½-inch cubes

1 To make the soup, heat the oil in a
large saucepan, add the onion and
carrots and cook gently for 5 minutes,
stirring occasionally. Add the ground
spices and cook gently for 1 minute,
continuing to stir.

2 Stir in the stock, bring to a boil,
then cover and cook gently, stirring
occasionally, for about 45 minutes,
until the carrots are tender.

3 Meanwhile, make the garlic
croutons. Heat a little oil in a
frying pan, add the garlic and cook
gently for 30 seconds, stirring. Add the
bread cubes, turn them over in the oil
and fry over medium heat, turning
frequently, for a few minutes, until
crisp and golden brown all over. Drain
on paper towels and keep warm.

4 Purée the soup in a blender or food
processor until smooth, then season
to taste with salt and pepper. Return
the soup to the rinsed-out saucepan
and reheat gently. Serve hot, sprinkled
with garlic croutons and garnished with
cilantro sprigs.

NUTRITION NOTES	
Per portion:	
Calories	127
Fat, total	6.1g
saturated fat	0.92g
Protein	2.65g
Carbohydrate	17.2g
sugar, total	7.74g
Fiber—NSP	2.94g
Sodium	626mg

Sweet Potato and Parsnip Soup

INGREDIENTS

Serves 6
1 tablespoon sunflower oil
1 large leek, sliced
2 celery ribs, chopped
1 pound sweet potatoes, diced
8 ounces parsnips, diced
3¾ cups vegetable or chicken stock
salt and ground black pepper
1 tablespoon chopped fresh parsley and
    roasted strips of sweet potatoes and
    parsnips, to garnish

1 Heat the oil in a large saucepan,
add the leek, celery, sweet potatoes
and parsnips. Cook gently for about
5 minutes, stirring to prevent them
from browning or sticking to the pan.

2 Stir in the vegetable or chicken
stock and bring to a boil, then
cover and simmer gently, stirring
occasionally, for about 25 minutes, or
until the vegetables are tender. Season
to taste with salt and pepper.

3 Remove the pan from the heat and
allow to cool slightly.

4 Purée the soup in a blender or food
processor until smooth, then return
the soup to the saucepan and reheat
gently. Ladle into warmed soup bowls
to serve and sprinkle with the chopped
fresh parsley and roasted strips of sweet
potatoes and parsnips to garnish.

NUTRITION NOTES	
Per portion:	
Calories	115
Fat, total	4g
saturated fat	0.46g
Protein	3.1g
Carbohydrate	17.9g
sugar, total	3.72g
Fiber—NSP	3.07g
Sodium	780mg

Fresh Mushroom Soup with Tarragon

This is a light mushroom soup subtly flavored with tarragon.

INGREDIENTS

Serves 6

1 tablespoon sunflower margarine
4 shallots, finely chopped
1 pound cremini mushrooms, finely chopped
1¼ cups vegetable stock
1¼ cups low-fat milk
1–2 tablespoons chopped fresh tarragon
2 tablespoons dry sherry (optional)
salt and ground black pepper
fresh tarragon sprigs, to garnish

— VARIATION —

Use a mixture of wild and button mushrooms instead of cremini mushrooms.

---

1 Melt the margarine in a large saucepan, add the shallots and cook gently for 5 minutes, stirring them occasionally. Add the mushrooms and cook gently for 3 minutes, stirring.

2 Stir in the stock and milk, bring to a boil, then cover and simmer gently for about 20 minutes, until the vegetables are soft. Stir in the chopped tarragon and season to taste with salt and pepper.

3 Allow the soup to cool slightly, then purée in a blender or food processor, in batches if necessary, until smooth. Return to the rinsed-out saucepan and reheat gently.

4 Stir in the sherry, if using, then ladle the soup into warmed soup bowls and serve garnished with tarragon sprigs.

— NUTRITION NOTES —

Per portion:

Calories	65
Fat, total	3.5g
saturated fat	1.2g
Protein	3.6g
Carbohydrate	3.9g
sugar, total	3.3g
Fiber—NSP	1g
Sodium	250mg

Prosciutto and Olive Bruschetta

A classic Italian snack, these appetizing toasts are ideal either on their own as finger food or as an appetizer served with a lightly dressed mixed green salad and accompanied by a glass of chilled white wine.

INGREDIENTS

Serves 4

4 slices of gluten-free bread
1 whole garlic clove, halved
a little olive oil, for drizzling
small handful of basil leaves
4 prosciutto slices
½ cup pitted black olives, roughly chopped
grated fresh Parmesan cheese, to serve (optional)

1 Toast the bread lightly on both sides until golden brown.

2 Cut larger slices of bread in half, if you like, then rub one side of each piece of toast with a cut side of the halved garlic clove.

— NUTRITION NOTES —

Per portion:

Calories	176
Fat, total	9.1g
saturated fat	3.4g
Protein	9.9g
Carbohydrate	13.7g
sugar, total	1.2g
Fiber—NSP	0.5g
Sodium	703mg

3 Drizzle a little olive oil over each slice of toast. Top with some basil leaves, then the slices of prosciutto, arranging the slices to fit the shape of the toast. Scatter the chopped black olives over the top.

4 Serve the bruschetta immediately, with a little grated Parmesan cheese sprinkled over them, if desired.

Bacon and Herb Rösti

INGREDIENTS

Serves 4

1 pound potatoes, left whole
   and unpeeled
2 tablespoons olive oil
1 red onion, finely chopped
4 lean bacon slices, diced
1 tablespoon potato flour
2 tablespoons chopped fresh
   mixed herbs
salt and ground black pepper
fresh parsley sprigs, to garnish

1 Lightly grease a baking sheet. Parboil the potatoes in a saucepan of lightly salted, boiling water for about 6 minutes. Drain the potatoes and set aside to cool slightly.

2 When cool enough to handle, peel the potatoes and coarsely grate them into a bowl. Set aside.

3 Heat 1 tablespoon of the oil in a frying pan, add the onion and bacon and cook gently for 5 minutes, stirring occasionally. Preheat the oven to 425°F.

4 Remove the pan from the heat. Stir the onion mixture, remaining oil, potato flour, herbs and seasoning into the grated potatoes and mix well.

5 Divide the mixture into eight small piles and spoon them onto the prepared baking sheet, leaving a little space between them.

6 Bake for 20–25 minutes, until the rösti are crisp and golden brown. Serve immediately, garnished with sprigs of fresh parsley.

NUTRITION NOTES	
Per portion:	
Calories	245
Fat, total	12.6g
saturated fat	2.9g
Protein	10.7g
Carbohydrate	23.6g
sugar, total	1.8g
Fiber—NSP	2.6g
Sodium	572mg

Grilled Vegetable Pizza

INGREDIENTS

Serves 6

1 zucchini, sliced
2 baby eggplants or 1 small
   eggplant, sliced
2 tablespoons olive oil
1 yellow bell pepper, seeded and
   thickly sliced
1 cup gluten-free cornmeal
½ cup potato flour
½ cup soy flour
1 teaspoon gluten-free baking powder
½ teaspoon salt
4 tablespoons soft margarine
about ½ cup low-fat milk
4 plum tomatoes, peeled
   and chopped
2 tablespoons chopped fresh basil
4 ounces mozzarella cheese, sliced
salt and ground black pepper
fresh basil sprigs, to garnish

1 Preheat the broiler. Brush the zucchini and eggplant slices with a little oil and place on a broiler rack with the pepper slices. Cook under the broiler until lightly browned, turning once.

2 Meanwhile, preheat the oven to 400°F. Place the cornmeal, potato flour, soy flour, baking powder and salt in a mixing bowl and stir to mix. Lightly rub in the margarine until the mixture resembles coarse bread crumbs, then stir in enough of the milk to make a soft but not sticky dough.

3 Place the dough on a sheet of baking parchment on a baking sheet and roll or press it out to form a 10-inch round, making the edges slightly thicker than the center.

4 Brush the pizza dough with any remaining oil, then spread the chopped tomatoes over the dough.

5 Sprinkle with the chopped basil and season with salt and pepper. Arrange the grilled vegetables over the tomatoes and top with the cheese.

6 Bake for 25–30 minutes, until crisp and golden brown. Garnish the pizza with fresh basil sprigs and serve immediately, cut into slices.

NUTRITION NOTES

Per portion:	
Calories	326
Fat, total	19.5g
saturated fat	5.8g
Protein	12.2g
Carbohydrate	26.8g
sugar, total	5.1g
Fiber—NSP	3.2g
Sodium	365mg

Warm Chicken Salad with Hazelnut Dressing

This simple warm salad combines panfried chicken and spinach with a light, nutty dressing.

INGREDIENTS

Serves 4

3 tablespoons olive oil
2 tablespoons hazelnut oil
1 tablespoon white wine vinegar
1 garlic clove, crushed
1 tablespoon chopped fresh mixed
  herbs
8 ounces baby spinach leaves
9 ounces cherry tomatoes, halved
1 bunch scallions, chopped
2 skinless, boneless chicken breasts, cut
  into thin strips

VARIATION

Use other meat or fish such as beef or salmon in place of the chicken.

1 First make the dressing. Place 2 tablespoons of the olive oil, the hazelnut oil, vinegar, garlic and chopped herbs in a small bowl or pitcher and whisk together until thoroughly mixed. Set aside.

2 Trim any long stalks from the spinach leaves, then place in a large serving bowl with the tomatoes and scallions and toss together to mix.

NUTRITION NOTES

Per portion:

Calories	300
Fat, total	20.9g
saturated fat	2.7g
Protein	23.2g
Carbohydrate	4.8g
sugar, total	4.5g
Fiber—NSP	2.4g
Sodium	126mg

3 Heat the remaining 1 tablespoon olive oil in a frying pan, add the chicken and stir-fry over high heat for 7–10 minutes, until the chicken is cooked, tender and lightly browned.

4 Scatter the cooked chicken pieces over the salad, give the dressing a quick whisk to blend, then drizzle it over the salad and gently toss all the ingredients together to mix. Season to taste with salt and pepper and serve immediately.

Fruit and Nut Coleslaw

A delicious and nutritious mixture of crunchy vegetables, fruit and nuts, tossed together in a light mayonnaise dressing.

INGREDIENTS

Serves 6

8 ounces white cabbage
1 large carrot
¾ cup dried apricots
2 ounces (½ cup) walnuts
2 ounces (½ cup) hazelnuts
4 ounces (1 cup) raisins
2 tablespoons chopped fresh parsley or
  chives or a mixture
7 tablespoons gluten-free reduced-
  calorie mayonnaise
5 tablespoons low-fat plain yogurt
salt and ground black pepper
fresh chives, to garnish

1 Finely shred the cabbage, coarsely grate the carrot and place both in a large mixing bowl. Roughly chop the apricots and nuts. Stir them into the cabbage and carrots with the raisins and chopped herbs.

2 In a separate bowl, mix together the mayonnaise and yogurt and season to taste with salt and pepper.

3 Add the mayonnaise to the cabbage mixture and toss together to mix.

4 Cover the bowl and set aside in a cool place for at least 30 minutes before serving, to allow the flavors to mingle. Serve the coleslaw garnished with a few fresh chives.

NUTRITION NOTES

Per portion:

Calories	283
Fat, total	16.4g
saturated fat	0.9g
Protein	5.5g
Carbohydrate	30.1g
sugar, total	29g
Fiber—NSP	4.4g
Sodium	199mg

Seafood and Herb Salad

Quick and easy to prepare, this warm mixed seafood salad makes a great lunchtime snack. Serve with baked potatoes for a more substantial meal.

INGREDIENTS

Serves 4

2 tablespoons olive oil
1 tablespoon flavored oil, such as basil oil or chile oil
finely grated rind of 1 small lemon
1 tablespoon lemon juice
1 garlic clove, crushed
2 tablespoons chopped fresh basil
6 ounces mixed salad greens
4 ounces sugar snap peas, chopped
14 ounces cooked mixed seafood, such as shrimp, scallops and squid
salt and ground black pepper

1 Place 1 tablespoon of the olive oil, the flavored oil, grated lemon rind, lemon juice, garlic and basil in a small bowl. Season with salt and pepper to taste and whisk together until thoroughly mixed. Set aside.

2 Place the salad greens and sugar snap peas in a serving bowl and toss lightly to mix.

--- NUTRITION NOTES ---

Per portion:

Calories	202
Fat, total	12.8g
saturated fat	1.8g
Protein	18.1g
Carbohydrate	3.8g
sugar, total	1.9g
Fiber—NSP	1.1g
Sodium	289mg

3 Heat the remaining olive oil in a large frying pan or wok, add the seafood and briefly stir-fry over medium heat. Scatter the seafood over the salad greens, drizzle the dressing over the salad, toss together to mix and serve.

--- VARIATION ---

Use the fresh cooked seafood of your choice instead of a mixture.

Citrus Fruit Salad

A refreshingly tangy combination —arugula and lamb's lettuce leaves are topped with fresh grapefruit, oranges and avocado in a light, fruity dressing.

INGREDIENTS

Serves 4

1 pink grapefruit
2 oranges
1 avocado
2 ounces (½ cup) pine nuts
5 tablespoons olive oil
2 teaspoons balsamic vinegar
2 tablespoons freshly squeezed orange juice
2 ounces lamb's lettuce (mâche)
2 ounces arugula
salt and ground black pepper
fresh herb sprigs, to garnish

1 Halve and segment the grapefruit and oranges and place the segments in a mixing bowl. Squeeze any juices into the bowl, if desired.

2 Peel and slice the avocado and add the slices to the bowl.

3 Gently stir in the pine nuts, taking care not to break up the avocado.

4 Whisk together the olive oil, vinegar, orange juice and seasoning in a small bowl and stir into the fruit mixture. Arrange the lamb's lettuce and arugula on four serving plates and spoon a little fruit and dressing over each. Garnish with herb sprigs and serve immediately.

--- NUTRITION NOTES ---

Per portion:

Calories	307
Fat, total	26.6g
saturated fat	3.56g
Protein	4.8g
Carbohydrate	12.8g
sugar, total	11.8g
Fiber—NSP	4.95g
Sodium	63mg

MEAT, POULTRY AND FISH

Meat, poultry or fish form the basis of many delicious gluten-free recipes and, when served with cooked potatoes, rice or rice noodles and seasonal fresh vegetables, make tasty, filling and healthy meals. The following tempting selection of recipes, which includes Pancetta and Fava Bean Risotto, Beef and Broccoli Stir-fry, Cod, Tomato and Pepper Casserole and Panfried Chicken with Pesto, will appeal to the whole family.

Pancetta and Fava Bean Risotto

This delicious risotto makes a healthy and filling meal, served with cooked fresh seasonal vegetables or a mixed green salad.

INGREDIENTS

Serves 4

1 tablespoon olive oil
1 onion, chopped
2 garlic cloves, finely chopped
6 ounces pancetta or bacon, diced
1¾ cups arborio rice
5 cups chicken stock
8 ounces frozen baby fava or lima beans
2 tablespoons chopped fresh mixed
    herbs, such as parsley, thyme
    and oregano
salt and ground black pepper
shavings of Parmesan cheese, to serve
chopped fresh flat-leaf parsley,
    to garnish

1 Heat the oil in a large saucepan or frying pan. Add the onion, garlic and pancetta or bacon and cook gently for about 5 minutes, stirring occasionally.

2 Add the rice to the pan and cook for 1 minute, stirring. Add 1¼ cups of the stock and simmer, stirring frequently, until it has been absorbed.

3 Continue adding the stock, a ladleful at a time, stirring frequently until the rice is al dente and creamy, and almost all the liquid has been absorbed. This will take 30–35 minutes. It may not be necessary to add all the stock.

4 Meanwhile, cook the beans in a saucepan of lightly salted, boiling water for about 3 minutes, until tender. Drain and keep warm.

5 Stir the beans, mixed herbs and seasoning into the risotto. Serve sprinkled with shavings of Parmesan cheese and garnished with parsley.

NUTRITION NOTES	
Per portion:	
Calories	485
Fat, total	9.9g
saturated fat	1.7g
Protein	22.35g
Carbohydrate	74.7g
sugar, total	1.93g
Fiber—NSP	4.36g
Sodium	1969mg

Pork Meatballs with Pasta

Serve these tasty meatballs on a bed of freshly cooked gluten-free pasta, such as corn spaghetti.

INGREDIENTS

Serves 6

1 pound lean ground pork
1 leek, finely chopped
4 ounces mushrooms, finely chopped
1 tablespoon chopped fresh thyme
1 tablespoon tomato paste
1 egg, beaten
2 tablespoons potato flour
1 tablespoon sunflower oil
12 ounces–1¼ pounds gluten-free pasta
fresh thyme sprigs, to garnish

For the tomato sauce

1 onion, finely chopped
1 carrot, finely chopped
1 celery rib, finely chopped
1 garlic clove, crushed
1½ pounds ripe tomatoes, peeled, seeded and chopped
⅔ cup dry white wine
⅔ cup flavorful vegetable stock
1 tablespoon tomato paste
1 tablespoon chopped fresh basil
salt and ground black pepper

1 Preheat the oven to 350°F. To make the meatballs, put the pork, leek, mushrooms, chopped thyme, tomato paste, egg and potato flour in a bowl and stir together until thoroughly mixed. Shape into small balls, place on a plate, cover and chill while making the tomato sauce.

2 Place all the sauce ingredients in a small saucepan, season to taste, then bring to a boil. Boil, uncovered, for 10 minutes, until thickened.

NUTRITION NOTES	
Per portion:	
Calories	504
Fat, total	8.8g
saturated fat	2.2g
Protein	26.5g
Carbohydrate	76.4g
sugar, total	6.9g
Fiber—NSP	2.5g
Sodium	295mg

3 Heat the oil in a frying pan, add the meatballs and cook in batches until lightly browned. Place them in a shallow ovenproof dish and pour the tomato sauce on top. Cover and bake for about 1 hour, until cooked through.

4 Meanwhile, cook the pasta in a pan of lightly salted, boiling water for 8–12 minutes, or according to the package instructions, until al dente. Rinse under boiling water and then drain.

5 Spoon the cooked pasta into warmed bowls, spoon the meatballs and sauce over the top and serve garnished with fresh thyme sprigs.

Braised Lamb with Apricots and Herb Dumplings

A rich and fruity lamb casserole, topped with light, herby gluten-free dumplings, which is delicious served with baked potatoes and broccoli.

INGREDIENTS

Serves 6

2 tablespoons sunflower oil
1½ pounds lean lamb fillet, cut into
    1-inch cubes
12 ounces pearl onions, peeled
1 garlic clove, crushed
8 ounces button mushrooms
¾ cup small dried apricots
1 cup flavorful lamb or beef stock
1 cup red wine
1 tablespoon tomato paste
salt and ground black pepper
fresh herb sprigs, to garnish

For the dumplings

1 cup gluten-free pancake and
    baking mix
scant ½ cup gluten-free vegetable
    shortening
1–2 tablespoons chopped fresh
    mixed herbs

VARIATIONS

Use lean beef or pork in place of the lamb and substitute shallots for the pearl onions, if you prefer.

NUTRITION NOTES

Per portion:

Calories	513
Fat, total	28.8g
saturated fat	11.6g
Protein	26.1g
Carbohydrate	31.6g
sugar, total	15.3g
Fiber—NSP	3.4g
Sodium	257mg

1 Preheat the oven to 325°F. Heat the oil in a large, flameproof casserole, add the lamb and cook gently until browned all over, stirring occasionally. Remove the meat from the casserole using a slotted spoon, set aside and keep warm.

2 Add the onions, garlic and mushrooms to the oil remaining in the casserole and cook gently for about 5 minutes, stirring occasionally.

3 Return the meat to the casserole, add the dried apricots, stock, wine and tomato paste. Season to taste with salt and pepper and stir to mix.

4 Bring to a boil, stirring, then remove the casserole from the heat and cover. Transfer the casserole to the oven and cook for 1½–2 hours, until the lamb is cooked and tender, stirring once or twice and adding a little extra stock, if necessary.

5 Meanwhile, make the dumplings. Place the baking mix, shortening, herbs and seasoning in a bowl and stir to mix. Add enough cold water to make a soft, elastic dough. Divide the dough into small, marble-size pieces and, using lightly floured hands, roll each piece into a small ball.

6 Remove the lid from the casserole and place the dumplings on top of the braised lamb and vegetables.

7 Increase the oven temperature to 375°F. Return the casserole to the oven and cook for another 20–25 minutes, until the herb dumplings are cooked. Serve, garnished with fresh herb sprigs.

Beef and Broccoli Stir-fry

A quick-to-make dish with Asian appeal.

INGREDIENTS

Serves 4

2 teaspoons gluten-free cornstarch
3 tablespoons gluten-free soy sauce
3 tablespoons ruby port
1 tablespoon sunflower oil
12 ounces lean beef steak, cut into
   thin strips
1 garlic clove, crushed
1-inch piece fresh ginger, peeled and
   finely chopped
1 red bell pepper, seeded and sliced
8 ounces small broccoli florets
salt and ground black pepper
fresh parsley sprigs, to garnish
herby brown rice or rice noodles,
   to serve

1 Blend the cornstarch with the soy sauce and port in a small bowl.

2 Heat the oil in a large frying pan or wok, add the beef, garlic and ginger and stir-fry over medium heat for 2–3 minutes, until the beef is browned all over. Add the red pepper and broccoli; stir-fry for 4–5 minutes, until the vegetables are just tender.

3 Add the cornstarch mixture and salt and pepper to the pan, then cook, stirring constantly, until the sauce thickens and becomes glossy. Lower the heat and stir-fry for 1 minute more. Serve at once, garnished with parsley sprigs and accompanied by herby brown rice or rice noodles.

NUTRITION NOTES	
Per portion:	
Calories	217
Fat, total	9.8g
saturated fat	3.0g
Protein	21.9g
Carbohydrate	7.4g
sugar, total	3.8g
Fiber—NSP	1.86g
Sodium	46mg

Panfried Chicken with Pesto

Panfried chicken, served with warm pesto, makes a delicious quick main course. Serve with gluten-free pasta or rice noodles and braised vegetables.

INGREDIENTS

Serves 4

1 tablespoon olive oil
4 skinless, boneless chicken breasts
fresh basil leaves, to garnish
braised baby carrots and celery,
   to serve

For the pesto
6 tablespoons olive oil
½ cup pine nuts
⅔ cup freshly grated Parmesan cheese
1 cup fresh basil leaves
¼ cup fresh parsley
2 garlic cloves, crushed
salt and ground black pepper

1 Heat the 1 tablespoon oil in a frying pan. Add the chicken breasts and cook gently for 15–20 minutes, turning several times, until the chicken breasts are tender, lightly browned and thoroughly cooked.

2 Meanwhile, make the pesto. Place the olive oil, pine nuts, Parmesan cheese, basil leaves, parsley, garlic and salt and pepper in a blender or food processor and process until smooth and well mixed.

3 Remove the chicken from the pan, cover and keep hot. Reduce the heat slightly, then add the pesto to the pan and cook gently, stirring constantly, for a few minutes, until the pesto has warmed through.

4 Pour the warm pesto over the chicken, then garnish with basil leaves and serve with braised baby carrots and celery.

NUTRITION NOTES	
Per portion:	
Calories	581
Fat, total	41.9g
saturated fat	7.67g
Protein	49.12g
Carbohydrate	1.97g
sugar, total	0.64g
Fiber—NSP	0.6g
Sodium	210mg

Thai Chicken and Vegetable Curry

For this curry, chicken and vegetables are cooked in a Thai-spiced coconut sauce.

INGREDIENTS

Serves 4

1 tablespoon sunflower oil
6 shallots, finely chopped
2 garlic cloves, crushed
1 pound skinless, boneless chicken
 breasts, cut into ½-inch cubes
1 teaspoon ground coriander
1 teaspoon ground cumin
4 teaspoons Thai green curry paste
1 green bell pepper, seeded and diced
6 ounces baby corn, halved
4 ounces green beans, halved
⅔ cup chicken stock
⅔ cup coconut milk
2 tablespoons gluten-free cornstarch
cilantro sprigs and toasted cashew nuts,
 to garnish
boiled rice, to serve

1 Heat the oil in a saucepan, add the shallots, garlic and chicken and cook for 5 minutes, stirring occasionally, until the chicken is colored all over.

2 Add the coriander, cumin and curry paste and cook for 1 minute.

3 Add the green pepper, baby corn, beans, stock and coconut milk and stir to mix.

4 Bring to a boil, stirring constantly, then cover and simmer for 20–30 minutes, stirring occasionally, until the chicken is tender.

--- COOK'S TIP ---

Add more Thai green curry paste for a hotter curry, if you like.

5 Blend the cornstarch with about 3 tablespoons water in a small bowl. Stir into the curry, then simmer gently for about 2 minutes, stirring constantly, until the sauce thickens slightly. Serve hot, garnished with fresh cilantro and toasted cashew nuts and accompanied by boiled rice.

--- NUTRITION NOTES ---

Per portion:
Calories	233
Fat, total	6.65g
saturated fat	0.93g
Protein	30.1g
Carbohydrate	14.1g
sugar, total	5g
Fiber—NSP	3.43g
Sodium	924mg

Chicken and Leek Pie

Crisp and light gluten-free pastry, flavored with fresh herbs, tops a tarragon-flavored chicken and leek sauce to make this tempting savory pie a popular choice.

INGREDIENTS

Serves 4

1½ cups gluten-free flour
pinch of salt
7 tablespoons sunflower margarine
1 tablespoon chopped fresh
 mixed herbs
3 leeks, sliced
3 tablespoons gluten-free cornstarch
1⅔ cups low-fat milk
1−2 tablespoons chopped
 fresh tarragon
12 ounces cooked skinless, boneless
 chicken breast, diced
7-ounce can corn kernels, drained
salt and ground black pepper
fresh herb sprigs and salt flakes,
 to garnish

1 Make the pastry. Place the flour and salt in a bowl and lightly rub in 6 tablespoons of the margarine until the mixture resembles bread crumbs. Stir in the mixed herbs and add a little cold water to make a smooth, firm dough. Wrap the pastry in a plastic bag and chill for 30 minutes.

2 Preheat the oven to 375°F. Steam the leeks for about 10 minutes, until just tender. Drain thoroughly and keep warm.

3 Meanwhile, blend the cornstarch with 5 tablespoons of the milk. Heat the remaining milk in a saucepan until it is just beginning to boil, then pour it onto the cornstarch mixture, stirring constantly. Return the mixture to the pan and heat gently, stirring constantly, until the sauce comes to a boil and thickens. Simmer gently, stirring, for about 2 minutes.

4 Add the remaining margarine to the pan with the chopped tarragon, leeks, chicken and corn. Season to taste with salt and pepper and mix together well.

NUTRITION NOTES

Per portion:	
Calories	598
Fat, total	24g
saturated fat	5.6g
Protein	37.2g
Carbohydrate	59.9g
sugar, total	9.2g
Fiber—NSP	2.27g
Sodium	265mg

5 Spoon the chicken mixture into a 5-cup pie dish and place the dish on a baking sheet. Roll out the pastry to a shape slightly larger than the pie dish. Lay it over the dish, and press to seal. Trim, decorate the top with the trimmings, if desired, and make a slit in the center.

6 Bake for 35−40 minutes, until the pastry is golden brown. Serve at once, sprinkled with herbs and salt.

VARIATION

Use half milk and half chicken or vegetable stock, if preferred.

Marinated Monkfish with Tomato Coulis

A light but flavorful dish, perfect for summertime eating and enjoying al fresco with a glass or two of chilled, fruity wine.

INGREDIENTS

Serves 4

2 tablespoons olive oil
finely grated zest and juice of 1 lime
2 tablespoons chopped fresh mixed herbs
1 teaspoon gluten-free Dijon mustard
4 skinless, boneless monkfish fillets
salt and ground black pepper
fresh herb sprigs, to garnish

For the coulis

4 plum tomatoes, peeled and chopped
1 garlic clove, chopped
1 tablespoon olive oil
1 tablespoon tomato paste
2 tablespoons chopped fresh oregano
1 teaspoon light brown sugar

1 Place the oil, lime zest and juice, herbs, mustard and salt and pepper in a small bowl and whisk together until thoroughly mixed.

2 Place the monkfish fillets in a shallow, nonmetallic container and pour the lime mixture over them. Turn the fish several times in the marinade to coat it. Cover and chill for 1–2 hours.

3 Meanwhile, make the coulis. Place all the coulis ingredients in a blender or food processor and process until smooth. Season to taste, then cover and chill until required.

4 Preheat the oven to 350°F. Using a slotted spoon, place each fish fillet on a sheet of waxed paper big enough to hold it in a parcel.

5 Spoon a little marinade over each piece of fish. Gather the paper loosely over the fish and fold over the edges to secure the parcel tightly. Place on a baking sheet.

6 Bake for 20–30 minutes, until the fish fillets are cooked, tender and just beginning to flake.

7 Carefully unwrap the parcels and serve the fish fillets immediately, with a little of the chilled coulis served alongside, garnished with a few fresh herb sprigs.

COOK'S TIP

The coulis can be served hot, if you prefer. Simply make as directed in the recipe and heat gently in a saucepan until almost boiling before serving.

— NUTRITION NOTES —	
Per portion:	
Calories	210
Fat, total	12.26g
saturated fat	1.82g
Protein	20.75g
Carbohydrate	4.72g
sugar, total	3.8g
Fiber—NSP	1g
Sodium	77mg

Baked Trout with Wild Mushrooms

INGREDIENTS

Serves 4

4 whole rainbow trout, cleaned
juice of 1 lemon
1 tablespoon chopped fresh parsley
2 tablespoons olive oil
2 shallots, finely chopped
1 garlic clove, crushed
12 ounces mixed fresh wild
    mushrooms, chopped
1 tablespoon ruby port or Madeira
2 tablespoons crème fraîche
salt and ground black pepper
chopped fresh parsley, to garnish

1 Preheat the oven to 350°F. Place the trout, side by side, in a lightly greased, shallow, ovenproof dish. Pour the lemon juice over them and sprinkle the parsley on top.

2 Cover with foil and bake for 30–40 minutes, until the fish is cooked, tender and beginning to flake.

3 Meanwhile, heat the oil in a frying pan, add the shallots and garlic and cook gently for 3–5 minutes, stirring occasionally, until the shallots have softened. Add the mushrooms and cook gently for about 5 minutes, stirring occasionally, until they are just cooked.

4 Add the port or Madeira, increase the heat and cook, stirring, for a few minutes, until most of the liquid has evaporated. Add the crème fraîche, season to taste with salt and pepper and mix well.

5 Place the cooked trout on four warmed serving plates and spoon a little of the mushroom sauce over each fish or on either side of it. Sprinkle a little chopped parsley over each fish and serve immediately.

NUTRITION NOTES	
Per portion:	
Calories	330
Fat, total	18.4g
saturated fat	3.9g
Protein	38.3g
Carbohydrate	1.92g
sugar, total	1.62g
Fiber—NSP	1.3g
Sodium	102mg

Charbroiled Salmon Steaks with Mango Salsa

INGREDIENTS

Serves 4

1 medium, ripe mango
4 ounces cucumber
2 scallions
2 tablespoons chopped cilantro
4 salmon steaks, each about 6 ounces
juice of 1 lemon or lime
salt and ground black pepper
cilantro sprigs and lemon
    wedges, to garnish

1 Make the mango salsa. Peel and pit the mango, finely chop the flesh and place in a bowl. Peel, seed and finely chop the cucumber; chop the scallions. Add to the mango with the cilantro and salt and pepper. Mix, cover and let stand for 30 minutes.

2 While the salsa is standing to allow the flavors to mingle, preheat an outdoor grill or your broiler. Place the salmon steaks on a rack and drizzle with the lemon or lime juice. Cook the salmon over a hot grill or under a moderate broiler for 6 minutes on each side, until the steaks are cooked, tender and just beginning to flake.

3 Transfer the salmon to serving plates, spoon some mango salsa alongside each steak and serve immediately, garnished with cilantro sprigs and lemon wedges.

NUTRITION NOTES	
Per portion:	
Calories	350
Fat, total	19.5g
saturated fat	3.4g
Protein	36.2g
Carbohydrate	7.84g
sugar, total	4.3g
Fiber—NSP	2g
Sodium	98mg

Tuna, Zucchini and Pepper Frittata

This nutritious Italian omelet is quick and easy to make. Serve it simply, with a lightly dressed mixed or green salad.

INGREDIENTS

Serves 4
1 tablespoon sunflower oil
1 onion, chopped
1 zucchini, thinly sliced
1 red bell pepper, seeded and sliced
4 eggs
2 tablespoons low-fat milk
7-ounce can tuna in water, drained
    and flaked
2 teaspoons dried herbes de Provence
½ cup grated Red Leicester or
    Cheddar cheese
salt and ground black pepper
mixed or green salad, to serve

1 Heat the oil in a nonstick frying pan, add the onion, zucchini and red bell pepper and cook for 5 minutes, stirring frequently.

2 Beat the eggs with the milk, add the flaked tuna and herbs and season with salt and pepper. Mix well.

3 Pour the egg mixture into the frying pan on top of the vegetables and cook over medium heat until the eggs are beginning to set. Pull the sides into the middle to allow the uncooked egg to run onto the pan, then continue cooking undisturbed until the frittata is golden brown underneath. Meanwhile, preheat the broiler.

4 Sprinkle the cheese over the top of the frittata and broil until the cheese has melted and the top is golden.

5 Cut the frittata into wedges and serve immediately with a mixed or greef salad.

NUTRITION NOTES	
Per portion:	
Calories	250
Fat, total	15.3g
saturated fat	5.2g
Protein	24g
Carbohydrate	4.7g
sugar, total	3.1g
Fiber—NSP	0.8g
Sodium	330mg

Cod, Tomato and Pepper Casserole

The wonderful sun-drenched flavors of the Mediterranean are brought together in this appetizing potato-topped casserole. Lightly cooked zucchini make a tasty accompaniment.

INGREDIENTS

Serves 4

1 pound potatoes, cut into
   thin slices
2 tablespoons olive oil
1 red onion, chopped
1 garlic clove, crushed
1 red bell pepper, seeded and diced
1 yellow bell pepper, seeded and diced
8 ounces mushrooms, sliced
14-ounce and 8-ounce cans
   chopped tomatoes
⅔ cup dry white wine
1 pound skinless, boneless cod fillet,
   cut into ¾-inch cubes
½ cup pitted black olives, chopped
1 tablespoon chopped fresh basil
1 tablespoon chopped fresh oregano
salt and ground black pepper
fresh oregano sprigs, to garnish
cooked zucchini, to serve

1 Preheat the oven to 400°F. Parboil the potatoes in a saucepan of lightly salted boiling water for 4 minutes. Drain thoroughly, then add 1 tablespoon of the oil and toss together to mix. Set aside.

2 Heat the remaining oil in a saucepan, add the onion, garlic and red and yellow bell peppers and cook for 5 minutes, stirring occasionally.

3 Stir in the mushrooms, tomatoes and wine, bring to a boil and boil rapidly for a few minutes, until the sauce has reduced slightly.

4 Add the fish, olives, herbs and seasoning to the tomato mixture.

5 Spoon the mixture into a lightly greased casserole and arrange the potato slices over the top, covering the fish mixture completely.

6 Bake, uncovered, for about 45 minutes, until the fish is cooked and tender and the potato topping is browned. Garnish with fresh oregano sprigs and serve with zucchini.

— NUTRITION NOTES —	
Per portion:	
Calories	336
Fat, total	10.6g
saturated fat	1.5g
Protein	26.5g
Carbohydrate	29.2g
sugar, total	9g
Fiber—NSP	4.6g
Sodium	424mg

VEGETARIAN DISHES

If you prefer to follow a vegetarian diet or to choose a vegetarian dish as an alternative to meat, this chapter has a collection of appetizing and nutritious, gluten-free recipes, such as Vegetable Moussaka, Provençal Stuffed Peppers, Herby Rice Pilaf and Wild Mushroom and Broccoli Tart. Serve the dishes with fresh gluten-free bread or pasta, potatoes or rice and a mixed green salad or cooked vegetables.

Vegetable Moussaka

This is a really flavorful vegetarian alternative to classic meat moussaka. Serve it with warm, gluten-free bread and a glass or two of rustic red wine.

INGREDIENTS

Serves 6

1 pound eggplants, sliced
4 ounces whole green lentils
2½ cups vegetable stock
1 bay leaf
3 tablespoons olive oil
1 onion, sliced
1 garlic clove, crushed
8 ounces mushrooms, sliced
14-ounce can chickpeas, rinsed
  and drained
14-ounce can chopped tomatoes
2 tablespoons tomato paste
2 teaspoons dried herbes de Provence
3 tablespoons water
1¼ cups plain yogurt
3 eggs
½ cup grated mature Cheddar cheese
salt and ground black pepper
flat-leaf parsley sprigs, to garnish

1 Sprinkle the eggplant slices with salt and place in a colander. Cover and leave for 30 minutes to allow the bitter juices to be extracted.

2 Meanwhile, place the lentils, stock and bay leaf in a saucepan. Cover, bring to a boil and simmer for about 20 minutes, until the lentils are just tender. Drain well and keep warm.

3 Heat 1 tablespoon of the oil in a large saucepan, add the onion and garlic and cook for 5 minutes, stirring. Stir in the lentils, mushrooms, chickpeas, tomatoes, tomato paste, herbs and water. Bring to a boil, cover and simmer gently for 10 minutes.

4 Preheat the oven to 350°F. Rinse the eggplant slices, drain and pat dry. Heat the remaining oil in a frying pan and fry the slices in batches for 3–4 minutes, turning once.

5 Season the lentil mixture with salt and pepper. Arrange a layer of eggplant slices in the bottom of a large, shallow, ovenproof dish or roasting pan, then spoon on a layer of the lentil mixture. Continue the layers until all the eggplant slices and lentil mixture are used up.

6 Beat together the yogurt, eggs and salt and pepper and pour the mixture into the dish. Sprinkle the grated cheese on top and bake for about 45 minutes, until the topping is golden brown and bubbling. Serve immediately, garnished with flat-leaf parsley sprigs.

NUTRITION NOTES	
Per portion:	
Calories	348
Fat, total	17.3g
saturated fat	4.4g
Protein	20.6g
Carbohydrate	29.5g
sugar, total	9g
Fiber—NSP	7.1g
Sodium	722mg

Rice Noodles with Vegetable Chili Sauce

INGREDIENTS

Serves 4

1 tablespoon sunflower oil
1 onion, chopped
2 garlic cloves, crushed
1 fresh red chile, seeded and
 finely chopped
1 red bell pepper, seeded and diced
2 carrots, finely chopped
6 ounces baby corn, halved
8-ounce can sliced bamboo shoots,
 rinsed and drained
14-ounce can red kidney beans, rinsed
 and drained
1¼ cups passata or tomato sauce
1 tablespoon gluten-free soy sauce
1 teaspoon ground coriander
9 ounces rice noodles
2 tablespoons chopped fresh cilantro
 or parsley
salt and ground black pepper
fresh parsley sprigs, to garnish

1 Heat the oil, add the onion, garlic, chile and red bell pepper and cook for 5 minutes, stirring. Stir in the carrots, corn, bamboo shoots, kidney beans, passata or tomato sauce, soy sauce and ground coriander.

COOK'S TIP

After handling chiles, wash your hands. Chiles contain volatile oils that can irritate and burn sensitive areas, such as the eyes, if they are touched.

2 Bring to a boil, then cover, reduce the heat, and simmer gently for 30 minutes, stirring occasionally, until the vegetables are tender. Season with salt and pepper to taste.

3 Meanwhile, place the noodles in a bowl and cover with boiling water. Stir with a fork and let stand for 3–4 minutes, or according to the package instructions. Rinse with boiling water and drain thoroughly.

4 Stir the cilantro or parsley into the sauce. Spoon the noodles onto warmed serving plates and top with the sauce. Garnish with parsley and serve.

NUTRITION NOTES	
Per portion:	
Calories	409
Fat, total	5.2g
saturated fat	0.6g
Protein	13.5g
Carbohydrate	77.3g
sugar, total	10.6g
Fiber—NSP	8.7g
Sodium	1156mg

Harvest Vegetable and Lentil Casserole

INGREDIENTS

Serves 6

1 tablespoon sunflower oil
2 leeks, sliced
1 garlic clove, crushed
4 celery ribs, chopped
2 carrots, sliced
2 parsnips, diced
1 sweet potato, diced
8-ounce rutabaga, diced
6 ounces whole brown or green lentils
1 pound tomatoes, peeled, seeded and
    chopped
1 tablespoon chopped fresh thyme
1 tablespoon chopped fresh marjoram
3¾ cups flavorful vegetable stock
1 tablespoon gluten-free cornstarch
salt and ground black pepper
fresh thyme sprigs, to garnish

1 Preheat the oven to 350°F. Heat the oil in a large flameproof casserole. Add the leeks, garlic and celery and cook over low heat for 3 minutes, stirring occasionally.

NUTRITION NOTES

Per portion:	
Calories	254
Fat, total	11g
saturated fat	0.15g
Protein	11.5g
Carbohydrate	37.8g
sugar, total	10.8g
Fiber—NSP	7.1g
Sodium	722mg

2 Add the carrots, parsnips, sweet potato, rutabaga, lentils, tomatoes, herbs, stock and seasoning. Stir well. Bring to a boil, stirring occasionally.

3 Cover and bake for about 50 minutes, until the vegetables and lentils are cooked and tender, removing the casserole from the oven and stirring the vegetable mixture once or twice during the cooking time.

4 Remove the casserole from the oven. Blend the cornstarch with 3 tablespoons water in a small bowl. Stir it into the casserole and heat gently, stirring constantly, until the mixture comes to a boil and thickens, then simmer gently, stirring, for 2 minutes.

5 Spoon the casserole onto warmed serving plates or into bowls and serve garnished with thyme sprigs.

Herby Rice Pilaf

A quick and easy dish to make, this simple pilaf is delicious to eat. Serve with a selection of cooked fresh seasonal vegetables such as broccoli florets, baby corn and carrots.

INGREDIENTS

Serves 4

8 ounces mixed brown basmati and
    wild rice
1 tablespoon olive oil
1 onion, chopped
1 garlic clove, crushed
1 teaspoon each ground cumin and
    ground turmeric
½ cup golden raisins
3 cups vegetable stock
2–3 tablespoons chopped fresh
    mixed herbs
salt and ground black pepper
fresh herb sprigs and ¼ cup pistachio
    nuts, chopped, to garnish

1 Wash the rice in a sieve under cold running water, then drain well. Heat the oil in a saucepan, add the onion and garlic and cook gently, stirring occasionally, for 5 minutes.

2 Add the spices and rice and cook gently for 1 minute, stirring. Stir in the raisins and stock, then bring to a boil, cover and simmer gently, stirring occasionally, for 20–25 minutes, until the rice is cooked and just tender and almost all the liquid has been absorbed.

3 Stir in the chopped mixed herbs and season to taste with salt and pepper. Spoon the pilaf into a warmed serving dish and garnish with fresh herb sprigs and a scattering of chopped pistachio nuts. Serve immediately.

NUTRITION NOTES	
Per portion:	
Calories	326
Fat, total	8.6g
saturated fat	0.15g
Protein	1.0g
Carbohydrate	56g
sugar, total	10.2g
Fiber—NSP	1.4g
Sodium	630mg

Cheese-topped Roasted Baby Vegetables

A simple way of serving baby vegetables that really brings out their flavor.

INGREDIENTS

Serves 6

2¼ pounds mixed baby vegetables,
    such as eggplants, onions or shallots,
    zucchini, corn and button
    mushrooms
1 red bell pepper, seeded and cut into
    large pieces
1–2 garlic cloves, finely chopped
1–2 tablespoons olive oil
2 tablespoons chopped fresh mixed herbs
8 ounces cherry tomatoes
1 cup coarsely grated mozzarella cheese
salt and ground black pepper
black olives, to serve (optional)

1 Preheat the oven to 425°F. Cut all the mixed baby vegetables in half lengthwise.

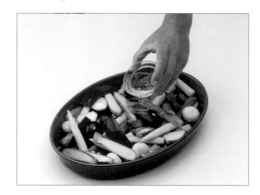

2 Place the baby vegetables and peppers in an ovenproof dish with the garlic and seasoning. Drizzle the oil over and toss the vegetables to coat them. Bake for 20 minutes, stirring once, until tinged brown at the edges.

3 Remove the dish from the oven and stir in the herbs. Scatter the tomatoes over the surface and top with the mozzarella cheese. Return to the oven and bake for 5–10 minutes more, until the cheese has melted and is bubbling. Serve at once, with black olives, if desired.

NUTRITION NOTES	
Per portion:	
Calories	162
Fat, total	10g
saturated fat	3.4g
Protein	8.2g
Carbohydrate	10.6g
sugar, total	7g
Fiber—NSP	3.1g
Sodium	172mg

Wild Mushroom and Broccoli Tart

Gluten-free potato and cheese pastry combines well with a mushroom and broccoli filling to make this savory tart a family favorite. Lightly cooked sliced leeks can be used instead of broccoli florets, if preferred.

INGREDIENTS

Serves 8

4 ounces small broccoli florets
1 tablespoon olive oil
3 shallots, finely chopped
6 ounces mixed wild mushrooms, such as cèpes, shiitake mushrooms and oyster mushrooms, sliced or chopped
2 eggs
scant 1 cup low-fat milk
1 tablespoon chopped fresh tarragon
½ cup grated Cheddar cheese
salt and ground black pepper
fresh herb sprigs, to garnish

For the pastry
¾ cup brown rice flour
¾ cup gluten-free cornmeal
pinch of salt
6 tablespoons soft margarine
4 ounces cold mashed potatoes
½ cup grated Cheddar cheese

2 Stir in the mashed potatoes and cheese and mix to form a smooth, soft dough. Wrap in a plastic bag and chill for 30 minutes.

3 Roll out the pastry between two sheets of waxed paper and use to line a 9½-inch removable-bottomed tart pan, gently pressing the pastry into the sides of the pan. Carefully trim around the top edge of the pastry shell with a sharp knife. Chill the pastry while making the filling.

1 First make the pastry. Place the rice flour, cornmeal and salt in a mixing bowl and stir to mix. Lightly rub in the margarine with your fingertips until the mixture resembles bread crumbs.

4 Preheat the oven to 400°F. Cook the broccoli florets in a saucepan of lightly salted, boiling water for 3 minutes. Drain thoroughly and set aside.

5 Heat the oil in a frying pan, add the shallots and cook gently, stirring, for 3 minutes. Add the mushrooms and cook for 2 minutes.

6 Spoon into the pastry shell and top with broccoli. Beat the eggs, milk, tarragon and seasoning together and pour over the vegetables. Top with cheese. Bake for 10 minutes, reduce the oven temperature to 350°F and bake for about 30 minutes, until lightly set. Serve warm or cold, garnished with fresh herbs.

Right: Savory Nut Loaf (top) and Wild Mushroom and Broccoli Tart.

NUTRITION NOTES	
Per portion:	
Calories	265
Fat, total	17.2g
saturated fat	5.54g
Protein	8.8g
Carbohydrate	18.5g
sugar, total	1.95g
Fiber—NSP	1g
Sodium	209mg

Savory Nut Loaf

This delicious nut loaf makes perfect picnic food.

INGREDIENTS

Serves 8

1 tablespoon olive oil
1 onion, chopped
1 leek, chopped
2 celery ribs, finely chopped
8 ounces mushrooms, chopped
2 garlic cloves, crushed
15-ounce can lentils, rinsed
   and drained
1 cup mixed nuts, such as hazelnuts,
   cashew nuts and almonds, finely
   chopped
2 ounces potato flour
½ cup grated mature Cheddar cheese
1 egg, beaten
3–4 tablespoons chopped fresh
   mixed herbs
salt and ground black pepper
flat-leaf parsley sprigs, to garnish

1 Preheat the oven to 375°F. Lightly grease and line the bottom and sides of a 13 x 4 x 4-inch loaf pan.

2 Heat the oil in a large saucepan, add the chopped onion, leek, celery and mushrooms and the crushed garlic, then cook gently, stirring occasionally, for 10 minutes, until the vegetables have softened.

3 Add the lentils, mixed nuts, potato flour, grated cheese, egg and herbs to the pan. Season with salt and pepper and mix thoroughly.

4 Spoon the nut, vegetable and lentil mixture into the prepared loaf pan and level the surface. Bake, uncovered, for 50–60 minutes, or until the nut loaf is lightly browned on top and firm to the touch.

5 Cool the loaf slightly in the pan, then turn it out onto a large serving plate. Serve hot or cold, cut into slices and garnished with flat-leaf parsley sprigs.

— NUTRITION NOTES —	
Per portion:	
Calories	230
Fat, total	13.1g
saturated fat	2.9g
Protein	12.5g
Carbohydrate	16.8g
sugar, total	1.9g
Fiber—NSP	4.3g
Sodium	67mg

Provençal Stuffed Peppers

INGREDIENTS

Serves 4

1 tablespoon olive oil
1 red onion, sliced
1 zucchini, diced
4 ounces mushrooms, sliced
1 garlic clove, crushed
14-ounce can chopped tomatoes
1 tablespoon tomato paste
scant ⅓ cup pine nuts
2 tablespoons chopped fresh basil
4 large peppers
½ cup finely grated Red Leicester or
   Cheddar cheese
salt and ground black pepper
fresh basil leaves, to garnish

1 Preheat the oven to 350°F. Heat the oil in a pan, add the onion, zucchini, mushrooms and garlic and cook gently for 3 minutes, stirring occasionally.

2 Stir in the tomatoes and tomato paste, then bring to a boil and simmer, uncovered, for 10–15 minutes, stirring occasionally, until thickened slightly. Remove from the heat and stir in the pine nuts, basil and seasoning.

3 Cut the peppers in half lengthwise and seed them. Blanch in a pan of boiling water for 3 minutes. Drain.

4 Place in a shallow, ovenproof dish and fill with the vegetable mixture.

5 Cover the dish with foil and bake for 20 minutes. Remove the foil, sprinkle each pepper with a little grated cheese and bake, uncovered, for another 5–10 minutes, until the cheese is melted and bubbling. Garnish with basil leaves and serve at once.

VARIATIONS

Use the vegetable sauce to stuff other vegetables, such as large zucchini or baby eggplants, in place of the peppers. Try grated Parmesan in place of Red Leicester.

NUTRITION NOTES

Per portion:
Calories	211
Fat, total	15.7g
saturated fat	3.8g
Protein	8.2g
Carbohydrate	10g
sugar, total	8.6g
Fiber—NSP	4.1g
Sodium	136mg

Mixed Mushroom and Parmesan Risotto

A classic risotto of mixed mushrooms, herbs and fresh Parmesan cheese, best simply served with a mixed green salad tossed in a light dressing.

INGREDIENTS

Serves 4

1 tablespoon olive oil
4 shallots, finely chopped
2 garlic cloves, crushed
¼ ounce dried porcini mushrooms, soaked in ⅔ cup hot water for 20 minutes
1 pound mixed wild mushrooms, such as portobello, cremini and shiitake mushrooms, sliced or chopped
9 ounces long-grain brown rice
3¾ cups flavorful vegetable stock
2–3 tablespoons chopped fresh flat-leaf parsley
⅔ cup grated Parmesan cheese
salt and ground black pepper

1 Heat the oil in a large saucepan, add the shallots and garlic and cook gently for 5 minutes, stirring. Drain the porcini, reserving their liquid, and chop roughly. Add all the mushrooms to the pan along with the porcini soaking liquid, the brown rice and 1¼ cups of the stock.

2 Bring to a boil, reduce the heat and simmer, uncovered, until all the liquid has been absorbed, stirring frequently. Add a ladleful of hot stock and stir until it has been absorbed.

3 Continue cooking and adding the hot stock, a ladleful at a time, until the rice is cooked and creamy but al dente, stirring frequently. This should take about 35 minutes and it may not be necessary to add all the stock.

4 Season with salt and pepper to taste, stir in the chopped parsley and grated Parmesan and serve at once. Alternatively, sprinkle the Parmesan over the risotto just before serving.

—— NUTRITION NOTES ——	
Per portion:	
Calories	358
Fat, total	10.9g
saturated fat	3.65g
Protein	12.8g
Carbohydrate	55.4g
sugar, total	2.2g
Fiber—NSP	3.4g
Sodium	738mg

Spring Vegetable Omelet

INGREDIENTS

Serves 4

2 ounces asparagus tips
2 ounces collard greens or chard, shredded
1 tablespoon sunflower oil
1 onion, sliced
6 ounces cooked new potatoes, halved or diced
2 tomatoes, chopped
6 eggs
1–2 tablespoons chopped fresh mixed herbs
salt and ground black pepper
salad, to serve

1 Steam the asparagus tips and greens over a saucepan of boiling water for 5–10 minutes, until tender. Drain the vegetables and keep warm.

2 Heat the oil in a large frying pan, add the onion and cook gently, stirring, for 5–10 minutes, until soft.

3 Add the new potatoes and cook for 3 minutes, stirring. Stir in the tomatoes, asparagus and greens. Lightly beat the eggs with the herbs and season with salt and pepper.

4 Pour the eggs over the vegetables, then cook over gentle heat until the bottom of the omelet is golden brown. Preheat the broiler to hot and cook the omelet under the broiler for 2–3 minutes, until the top is golden brown. Serve with salad.

—— NUTRITION NOTES ——	
Per portion:	
Calories	221
Fat, total	14.2g
saturated fat	3.4g
Protein	13.6g
Carbohydrate	10.4g
sugar, total	3.4g
Fiber—NSP	2.1g
Sodium	142mg

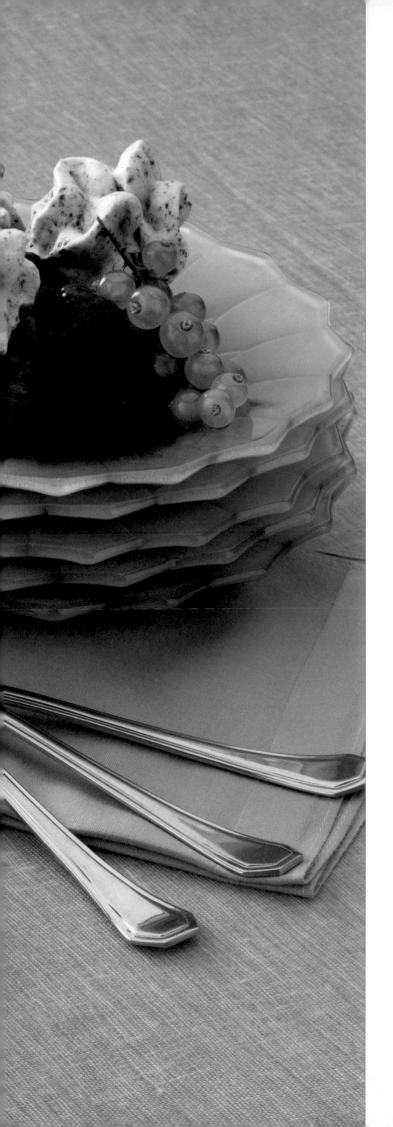

DESSERTS

Desserts are often the most tempting part of a meal, but they don't have to be naughty to be nice! These delicious and healthy gluten-free desserts include special occasion treats, such as Summer Strawberry Roulade and a rich chocolate mousse served with glazed kumquats, and scrumptious family fare, such as Creamy Lemon Rice Pudding and Mango Yogurt Ice. Plain yogurt, fromage frais, gluten-free custard, dairy cream or crème fraîche make excellent accompaniments.

Creamy Lemon Rice Pudding

This is a creamy baked rice pudding with a difference, being subtly flavored with lemon. It is wonderful served warm or cold with fresh strawberries.

INGREDIENTS

Serves 4

¼ cup short-grain white rice
2½ cups low-fat milk
2 tablespoons sugar
finely grated zest of 1 lemon
1 tablespoon butter, cut into
    small pieces
pared orange and lemon zest,
    to decorate

For serving

8 ounces prepared fresh fruit, such
    as strawberries or pineapple
6 tablespoons reduced-fat crème
    fraîche (optional)

1 Lightly grease a 1-quart ovenproof dish. Add the rice and pour in the milk, then set aside for about 30 minutes, to allow the rice to soften a little. Preheat the oven to 300°F.

2 Add the sugar, grated lemon zest and butter to the rice and milk and stir gently to mix. Bake for 2–2½ hours, until the top of the pudding is lightly browned.

3 Decorate with pared orange and lemon zest and serve warm or cold with the fresh fruit.

4 If serving cold, allow the pudding to cool, remove and discard the skin, then chill. Fold in the crème fraîche just before serving, if desired.

NUTRITION NOTES	
Per portion:	
Calories	220
Fat, total	8.8g
saturated fat	3.9g
Protein	6.8g
Carbohydrate	30.4g
sugar, total	19.7g
Fiber—NSP	0.7g
Sodium	121mg

Peach and Raspberry Crumble

INGREDIENTS

Serves 4

¾ cup brown rice flour
4 tablespoons soft margarine
¼ cup buckwheat flakes
¼ cup millet flakes
¼ cup hazelnuts, roughly chopped
scant ⅓ cup light brown sugar
1 teaspoon ground ginger
3 fresh peaches, pitted and cut
    into wedges
1⅓ cups raspberries
4 tablespoons fresh orange juice

1 Preheat the oven to 350°F. Grease a 5-cup pie dish. Place the rice flour in a bowl and rub in the margarine until the mixture resembles bread crumbs.

2 Stir in the buckwheat flakes, millet flakes, hazelnuts, ¼ cup of the sugar and the ginger. Mix well.

3 Mix the peaches, raspberries, orange juice and remaining sugar together and place in the dish. Sprinkle the crumble over the top, pressing it down lightly. Bake for 30–45 minutes, until the crumble is lightly browned. Serve warm or cold.

VARIATIONS
Use almonds or walnuts in place of the hazelnuts and substitute ground cinnamon for the ground ginger.
Firm, ripe nectarines or thinly sliced dessert apples could be used in place of the peaches, if you like.

NUTRITION NOTES	
Per portion:	
Calories	369
Fat, total	14.4g
saturated fat	2.5g
Protein	4.8g
Carbohydrate	57.5g
sugar, total	31.8g
Fiber—NSP	3.1g
Sodium	108mg

Summer Strawberry Roulade

INGREDIENTS

Serves 8

3 eggs
½ cup sugar, plus 2 tablespoons extra
   for sprinkling
1 cup gluten-free flour
½ cup Mediterranean-style yogurt
½ cup plain fromage frais
2 cups strawberries, sliced
strawberries and sprigs of mint,
   to decorate

1 Preheat the oven to 400°F. Place the eggs and the ½ cup sugar in a large bowl over a pan of simmering water. Beat, using an electric mixer, until the mixture is pale, creamy and thick enough to leave a trail on the surface when the beater is lifted.

2 Remove the bowl from the heat and beat the mixture until cool. Sift half the flour over it, then fold in gently using a metal spoon. Sift the remaining flour over and fold in with 1 tablespoon hot water.

3 Pour mixture into a greased and lined 13 x 9-inch jelly roll pan, tilting the pan to level the surface.

4 Bake for 10–15 minutes, or until well risen, golden brown and firm to the touch. Meanwhile, sprinkle a sheet of baking parchment with the remaining 2 tablespoons sugar. Turn out the hot cake onto the paper, trim off the crusty edges and quickly roll up the cake with the paper inside. Place seam side down on a wire rack and allow to cool completely.

5 Once it has cooled, carefully unroll the cake. Mix together the yogurt and fromage frais and spread evenly over the cake. Scatter the sliced strawberries over the top. Carefully reroll the cake and serve immediately, in slices, garnished with strawberries and sprigs of mint.

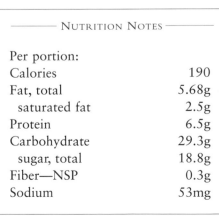

NUTRITION NOTES	
Per portion:	
Calories	190
Fat, total	5.68g
saturated fat	2.5g
Protein	6.5g
Carbohydrate	29.3g
sugar, total	18.8g
Fiber—NSP	0.3g
Sodium	53mg

Apple and Cinnamon Buckwheat Pancakes

Spiced panfried apple slices create a scrumptious topping for these buckwheat pancakes.

INGREDIENTS

Serves 4
3 cooking apples, peeled, cored
  and sliced
¼ cup sugar
4 tablespoons unsalted butter
2–3 tablespoons brandy
1–2 teaspoons ground cinnamon
fresh mint sprigs, to garnish
crème fraîche, to serve

For the pancakes
½ cup buckwheat flour
½ cup rice flour
pinch of salt
1 egg
1½ cups low-fat milk
sunflower oil, for frying

1 Make the pancakes. Place the buckwheat flour, rice flour and salt in a bowl and make a well in the center of the flour. Break in the egg and add a little of the milk, beating well with a wooden spoon.

2 Gradually beat in the remaining milk, drawing the flour in from the sides to make a smooth batter.

3 Heat a little oil in a 7-inch nonstick frying pan. Pour in enough batter to coat the bottom of the pan thinly. Cook until golden brown, then turn and cook on the other side.

4 Transfer the cooked pancake to a warmed plate and keep hot. Repeat with the remaining batter to make eight pancakes in all. Place the cooked pancakes on top of one another with waxed paper in between to prevent them from sticking together.

5 Toss the apple slices in the sugar in a mixing bowl.

6 Melt the butter in a large frying pan, add the apple slices to the pan and cook over high heat for about 5 minutes, stirring frequently, until the apple slices soften slightly and the sugar has caramelized. Remove the pan from the heat and sprinkle the apples with the brandy and cinnamon.

7 Serve the pancakes topped with the cooked apples and accompanied by some crème fraîche sprinkled with a little extra ground cinnamon, if desired, and garnished with mint.

— VARIATION —

Use pears in place of the apples and apple-pie spice instead of the cinnamon.

NUTRITION NOTES	
Per portion:	
Calories	368
Fat, total	16.1g
saturated fat	3.6g
Protein	6.5g
Carbohydrate	47.8g
sugar, total	27.3g
Fiber—NSP	1.7g
Sodium	151mg

Chocolate Meringues with Mixed Fruit Compote

Mini chocolate meringues are sandwiched with crème fraîche and served with a compote of mixed summer berries to make this impressive dessert.

INGREDIENTS

Serves 6

7 tablespoons unsweetened red
  grape juice
7 tablespoons unsweetened apple juice
2 tablespoons honey
1 pound mixed fresh berries, such as
  black currants, red currants,
  raspberries and blackberries

For the meringues

3 egg whites
¾ cup superfine sugar
3 ounces good-quality semisweet
  chocolate, finely grated
¾ cup reduced-fat
  crème fraîche

NUTRITION NOTES	
Per portion:	
Calories	292
Fat, total	9.48g
saturated fat	5.7g
Protein	3.8g
Carbohydrate	51.2g
sugar, total	51.1g
Fiber—NSP	1.7g
Sodium	49.8mg

1 Preheat the oven to 225°F. Line two baking sheets with baking parchment.

2 Make the meringues. Beat the egg whites in a large bowl until stiff. Gradually beat in half the sugar, then fold in the remaining sugar, using a metal spoon. Gently fold in the grated chocolate.

3 Spoon the meringue mixture into a large pastry bag fitted with a large star nozzle. Pipe small rounds onto the prepared baking sheets.

4 Bake for 2½–3 hours, until the meringues are firm and crisp, then transfer to a wire rack to cool.

5 Meanwhile, make the compote. Heat the fruit juices in a saucepan with the honey until almost boiling.

6 Place the mixed fresh berries in a large bowl and pour the hot fruit juice and honey mixture over them. Stir gently to mix, then set aside and let cool. Once cool, cover the bowl and chill until required.

7 When ready to serve, sandwich the cold meringues with the crème fraîche and arrange them on a serving plate or dish.

8 Serve the meringues immediately on individual plates with the mixed fruit compote.

Rich Chocolate Mousse with Glazed Kumquats

INGREDIENTS

Serves 6

8 ounces semisweet chocolate, broken
   into squares
4 eggs, separated
2 tablespoons brandy or orange liqueur
6 tablespoons heavy cream

For the glazed kumquats
10 ounces kumquats
½ cup sugar
1 tablespoon orange liqueur

1 Make the glazed kumquats. Slice the fruit and place cut face up in a shallow serving dish.

2 Place the sugar in a saucepan with ⅔ cup water. Heat gently, stirring constantly, until the sugar has dissolved, then bring to a boil and boil rapidly, without stirring, until a golden-brown caramel forms.

3 Remove the pan from the heat and very carefully stir in ¼ cup boiling water to dissolve the caramel. Stir in the orange liqueur, then pour the caramel over the kumquat slices and allow to cool. Once completely cool, cover and chill.

4 Make the chocolate mousse. Line a shallow 8-inch round cake pan with plastic wrap. Melt the chocolate in a bowl over a pan of simmering water, then remove the bowl from the heat.

5 Beat the egg yolks and brandy or liqueur into the chocolate, then fold in the cream, mixing well. In a separate clean bowl, beat the egg whites until stiff, then gently fold them into the chocolate mixture.

6 Pour the mixture into the prepared pan and level the surface. Chill for several hours, until set.

7 To serve, turn the mousse out onto a plate and cut into slices or wedges. Serve the chocolate mousse on serving plates and spoon some of the glazed kumquats alongside.

VARIATION

Use peeled and sliced small, seedless oranges in place of the kumquats.

NUTRITION NOTES

Per portion:	
Calories	432
Fat, total	22.3g
saturated fat	12g
Protein	7.6g
Carbohydrate	50.2g
sugar, total	49.8g
Fiber—NSP	2.68g
Sodium	68mg

Lemon Cheesecake with Wild Berries

INGREDIENTS

Serves 8

4 tablespoons unsalted butter
2 tablespoons light brown sugar
3 tablespoons golden syrup or light
   corn syrup
generous 1 cup gluten-free cornflakes
¼-ounce package powdered gelatin
8 ounces (1 cup) medium-fat soft
   cheese, such as cream cheese
generous ½ cup Mediterranean-style
   yogurt
⅔ cup half-and-half
finely grated zest and juice of 2 lemons
scant ½ cup granulated sugar
2 eggs, separated
confectioners' sugar, for dusting
8 ounces mixed fresh wild berries, such
   as blackberries, raspberries and red
   currants, to decorate

1 Place the butter, brown sugar and syrup in a saucepan and heat, stirring, over low heat until the mixture has melted and is well blended. Remove from the heat and stir in the cornflakes.

2 Press the mixture over the bottom of a deep 8-inch removable-bottomed round cake pan. Chill for 30 minutes.

3 Sprinkle the gelatin over 3 tablespoons water in a bowl and let soak for a few minutes. Place the bowl over a pan of simmering water and stir until the gelatin has dissolved. Place the cheese, yogurt, half-and-half, lemon zest and juice, granulated sugar and egg yolks in a large bowl and beat until smooth and thoroughly mixed.

4 Add the hot gelatin to the cheese and lemon mixture and beat until well mixed.

5 Beat the egg whites until stiff, then fold into the cheese mixture.

6 Pour the cheese mixture over the cornflake base and gently level the surface. Chill for 4–5 hours, until the filling has set. Carefully remove the cheesecake from the pan and place on a serving plate. Decorate with the mixed berries, dust with confectioners' sugar and serve immediately, in slices.

— VARIATION —

Use unsweetened puffed rice cereal or rice crispies in place of the cornflakes.

— NUTRITION NOTES —

Per portion:

Calories	297
Fat, total	15.2g
saturated fat	6.65g
Protein	8.9g
Carbohydrate	33.2g
sugar, total	22g
Fiber—NSP	0.9g
Sodium	267mg

Baked Fruit Compote

INGREDIENTS

Serves 6

⅔ cup dried figs
½ cup dried apricots
½ cup dried apple rings
¼ cup prunes
½ cup dried pears
½ cup dried peaches
1¼ cups unsweetened apple juice
1¼ cups unsweetened orange juice
6 cloves
1 cinnamon stick
toasted flaked almonds, to decorate

1 Preheat the oven to 350°F. Place the figs, apricots, apple rings, prunes, pears and peaches in a shallow ovenproof dish and stir to mix.

2 Mix together the apple and orange juices and pour over the fruit. Add the cloves and cinnamon stick and stir gently to mix.

3 Bake for about 30 minutes, until the fruit mixture is hot, stirring once or twice during cooking. Set aside and let soak for 20 minutes, then remove and discard the cloves and cinnamon stick.

4 Spoon into serving bowls and serve warm or cold, decorated with toasted flaked almonds.

> **COOK'S TIP**
> Use other mixtures of unsweetened fruit juices, such as pineapple and orange or grape and apple.

> **NUTRITION NOTES**
>
> Per portion:
>
> | | |
> |---|---|
> | Calories | 174 |
> | Fat, total | 0.8g |
> | saturated fat | 0.05g |
> | Protein | 2.5g |
> | Carbohydrate | 42.2g |
> | sugar, total | 42.1g |
> | Fiber—NSP | 5.16g |
> | Sodium | 26mg |

Mango Yogurt Ice

INGREDIENTS

Serves 6

1 pound ripe mango flesh, chopped
1¼ cups low-fat peach or apricot yogurt
⅔ cup Mediterranean-style yogurt
⅔ cup low-fat plain yogurt
2–4 tablespoons sugar
fresh mint sprigs, to decorate

1 Place the mango flesh in a blender or food processor and blend until smooth. Transfer to a bowl.

2 Add all three yogurts and blend until thoroughly mixed.

3 Stir in enough of the sugar to sweeten to taste and stir to mix.

4 Pour the mixture into a shallow plastic container. Cover and chill for 1½–2 hours, until it is mushy in consistency. Turn the mixture into a chilled bowl and beat until smooth.

5 Return the mixture to the plastic container, cover and freeze until the ice is firm. Transfer the ice to the refrigerator about 30 minutes before serving to allow it to soften a little. Serve in scoops decorated with mint sprigs.

> **NUTRITION NOTES**
>
> Per portion:
>
> | | |
> |---|---|
> | Calories | 155 |
> | Fat, total | 2.9g |
> | saturated fat | 1.7g |
> | Protein | 5.3g |
> | Carbohydrate | 28.4g |
> | sugar, total | 24.3g |
> | Fiber—NSP | 2.17g |
> | Sodium | 89.6mg |

Apricot and Almond Tart

Flaky, rich gluten-free pastry encases an apricot and almond filling to make this tempting dessert. Serve with Mediterranean-style yogurt or crème fraîche.

INGREDIENTS

Serves 6
½ cup (8 tablespoons) soft margarine
½ cup sugar
1 egg, beaten
⅓ cup ground rice
½ cup ground almonds
few drops of almond extract
1 pound fresh apricots, halved and pitted
sifted confectioners' sugar, for dusting
apricot slices and fresh mint sprigs, to decorate (optional)

For the pastry
1 cup brown rice flour
1 cup gluten-free cornmeal
pinch of salt
½ cup (8 tablespoons) soft margarine
2 tablespoons sugar
1 egg yolk

1 To make the pastry, place the rice flour, cornmeal and pinch of salt in a bowl and stir to mix. Lightly rub in the soft margarine until the mixture resembles bread crumbs.

─── VARIATION ───

For a change, use ground hazelnuts and vanilla extract in place of the ground almonds and almond extract.

2 Add the 2 tablespoons sugar, stir in the egg yolk and add enough chilled water to make a smooth, soft but not sticky dough. Wrap the dough and chill for 30 minutes.

3 Preheat the oven to 350°F. Line a 9½-inch removable-bottomed tart pan with the pastry by pressing it gently over the bottom and up the sides of the pan, making sure there are no holes in the pastry. Trim the edge with a sharp knife.

4 To make the almond filling, place the margarine and sugar in a mixing bowl and cream together, using a wooden spoon, until the mixture is light and fluffy.

5 Gradually add the beaten egg, beating well after each addition. Fold in the ground rice and almonds and the almond extract and mix well to incorporate them.

6 Spoon the almond mixture into the pastry shell, spreading it evenly, and arrange the apricot halves over the top, cut side down.

7 Place on a baking sheet and bake for 40–45 minutes, until the filling and pastry are cooked and lightly browned. Serve warm or cold, dusted with confectioners' sugar and decorated with apricots and sprigs of mint, if you like.

─── NUTRITION NOTES ───	
Per portion:	
Calories	487
Fat, total	29.6g
saturated fat	5.67g
Protein	5.6g
Carbohydrate	50.4g
sugar, total	22.8g
Fiber—NSP	1.54g
Sodium	212mg

BREADS, CAKES AND OTHER BAKED GOODS

The aroma wafting from the oven when baking homemade breads and cakes is hard to resist. These wonderful recipes are all gluten-free—try Cheese and Onion Corn Bread, a fabulous Victoria Layer Cake or Gingerbread and Country Apple Cake, or bake a batch of mouthwatering Apricot and Orange Muffins or Chocolate Chip Cookies, which make ideal treats and snacks for children and adults alike. Choose from this tempting selection and get baking!

Rice, Buckwheat and Corn Bread

Freshly baked, this wonderful bread is delicious served straight from the oven. Cut into thick slices and serve with fruit conserve or honey for breakfast.

INGREDIENTS

Makes one 2-pound loaf

scant 1 cup tepid low-fat milk
scant 1 cup tepid water
3 cups brown rice flour
½ cup buckwheat flour or soy flour
½ cup gluten-free cornmeal
1 teaspoon sugar
1 teaspoon salt
¼-ounce envelope active dry yeast
3 tablespoons soft margarine
1 medium egg, beaten, plus extra
   for glazing
2 tablespoons sesame seeds

COOK'S TIP

You can bake the bread in a different-shaped pan, such as a deep round or square cake pan, if preferred.

NUTRITION NOTES

Per loaf:

Calories	2,200
Fat, total	59g
saturated fat	12g
Protein	62g
Carbohydrate	344g
sugar, total	21g
Fiber—NSP	14g
Sodium	493mg

1 Lightly grease a 13 x 4 x 4-inch loaf pan. Mix the milk and water together in a measuring cup.

2 Place the rice flour, buckwheat or soy flour, cornmeal, sugar and salt in a bowl and stir in the yeast. Mix well until all the ingredients are combined, then lightly rub in the margarine until the mixture resembles fine bread crumbs.

3 Add the milk and water mixture and the egg and beat together to form a smooth, thick consistency.

4 Spoon the mixture into the prepared pan, then cover and let sit in a warm place until it has risen to the top of the pan.

5 Preheat the oven to 400°F. Brush the top of the bread with a little beaten egg and scatter the sesame seeds over it. Bake for about 30 minutes, until lightly browned. Run a knife all around the edge of the pan to loosen the loaf.

6 Turn out the bread onto a wire rack to cool slightly and serve warm. Alternatively, leave on the rack until completely cool, then cut into slices. To store, wrap in the loaf in foil or seal in a plastic bag.

Cheese and Onion Corn Bread

Full of flavor, this gluten-free corn bread is delicious served freshly baked, warm or cold, in slices, either on its own or spread with a little low-fat spread. It makes an ideal accompaniment to soups, stews and chilies.

INGREDIENTS

Makes one 2-pound loaf

1 tablespoon sunflower oil
1 onion, thinly sliced
1½ cups gluten-free cornmeal
¾ cup rice flour
¼ cup soy flour
1 tablespoon gluten-free baking powder
1 teaspoon sugar
1 teaspoon salt
4 ounces (1 cup) coarsely grated mature Cheddar cheese
scant 1 cup tepid milk
2 eggs
3 tablespoons soft margarine, melted

COOK'S TIP

Reserve a little of the grated cheese and cooked onion and sprinkle it over the top of the bread before baking.

1 Preheat the oven to 375°F. Lightly grease a 13 x 4 x 4-inch loaf pan. Heat the oil in a frying pan, add the onion and cook gently for 10–15 minutes, until softened, stirring occasionally. Remove from the heat and set aside to cool.

2 Place the cornmeal, rice flour, soy flour, baking powder, sugar and salt in a bowl and combine thoroughly. Stir in the cheese, mixing well.

3 Beat together the milk, eggs and melted margarine. Add to the flour mixture and mix well.

4 Stir in the cooled cooked onions and mix again.

5 Spoon the onion mixture into the prepared pan, level the surface and bake for about 30 minutes, until the bread has risen and is golden brown.

6 Run a knife around the edge to loosen the loaf. Turn out onto a wire rack to cool slightly and serve warm. Alternatively, leave it on the rack until completely cool, then cut into slices. To store the loaf, wrap it in foil or seal in a plastic bag.

NUTRITION NOTES

Per loaf:

Calories	2,314
Fat, total	121g
saturated fat	42g
Protein	83g
Carbohydrate	220g
sugar, total	21.2g
Fiber—NSP	9g
Sodium	3,100mg

Golden Raisins and Cinnamon Chewy Bars

These spicy, chewy bars are hard to resist and make a great treat, especially for children.

INGREDIENTS

Makes 16
½ cup (8 tablespoons) soft margarine
2 tablespoons light brown sugar
1 ounce plain toffees
¼ cup honey
1½ cups golden raisins
2 teaspoons ground cinnamon
6 ounces gluten-free rice crispies

1 Lightly grease a shallow 9 x 11-inch cake pan. Place the margarine, sugar, toffees and honey in a saucepan and heat gently, stirring, until melted. Bring to a boil, then remove the pan from the heat.

2 Stir in the raisins, cinnamon and rice crispies and mix well. Transfer the mixture to the prepared pan and spread the mixture evenly, pressing it down firmly.

3 Allow to cool, then chill until firm. Once firm, cut into bars, remove from the pan and serve. Store the bars in an airtight container in the refrigerator.

---- NUTRITION NOTES ----

Per bar:

Calories	145
Fat, total	6.4g
saturated fat	1.4g
Protein	1g
Carbohydrate	22.4g
sugar, total	13.4g
Fiber—NSP	0.3g
Sodium	1.95mg

Apricot and Orange Muffins

Serve these fruity muffins freshly baked and warm.

INGREDIENTS

Makes 8 large or 12 medium muffins
1 cup gluten-free cornmeal
¾ cup rice flour
1 tablespoon gluten-free baking powder
pinch of salt
4 tablespoons soft margarine, melted
¼ cup light brown sugar
1 egg, beaten
scant 1 cup low-fat milk
finely grated zest of 1 orange
½ cup dried apricots, chopped

1 Preheat the oven to 400°F. Lightly grease or line an 8- or 12-cup muffin pan. Place the cornmeal, rice flour, baking powder and salt in a bowl and mix.

2 Stir together the melted margarine, sugar, egg, milk and orange zest, then pour the mixture over the dry ingredients. Fold the ingredients gently together—just enough to combine them. The mixture will look quite lumpy, which is correct, as overmixing will result in heavy muffins.

3 Fold in the chopped dried apricots, then spoon the mixture into the prepared muffin pan, dividing it equally among the cups.

4 Bake for 15–20 minutes, until the muffins have risen and are golden brown and springy to the touch. Turn them out onto a wire rack to cool.

5 Serve the muffins warm or cold, on their own or cut in half and spread with a little low-fat spread. Store in an airtight container for up to one week or seal in plastic bags and freeze for up to three months.

---- NUTRITION NOTES ----

Per medium muffin:

Calories	136
Fat, total	4.6g
saturated fat	1g
Protein	2.9g
Carbohydrate	21g
sugar, total	8.5g
Fiber—NSP	0.9g
Sodium	195mg

Sponge Layer Cake

Serve this light, gluten-free equivalent of the classic sponge cake sandwiched together with your favorite jam. For special occasions, fill the cake with prepared fresh fruit, such as raspberries or sliced peaches, as well as jam and whipped dairy cream or fromage frais.

INGREDIENTS

Makes one 7-inch cake
¾ cup (12 tablespoons) soft margarine
¾ cup sugar
3 eggs, beaten
1½ cups gluten-free pancake and
  baking mix, sifted
4 tablespoons jam
⅔ cup whipped cream or fromage frais
1–2 tablespoons confectioners' sugar,
  for dusting

NUTRITION NOTES	
Per cake:	
Calories	3,140
Fat, total	166g
saturated fat	36g
Protein	35g
Carbohydrate	391g
sugar, total	263g
Fiber—NSP	0g
Sodium	1,486mg

1 Preheat the oven to 350°F. Lightly grease and line the bottom of two 7-inch cake pans.

2 Place the margarine and sugar in a bowl and cream together until pale and fluffy.

3 Add the eggs, a little at a time, beating well after each addition. Fold in half the baking mix, using a metal spoon, then fold in the rest.

VARIATION
Replace 2 tablespoons of the baking mix with sifted gluten-free cocoa powder. Sandwich the cakes with chocolate butter icing.

4 Divide the mixture evenly between the two cake pans and level the surfaces with the back of a spoon.

5 Bake for 25–30 minutes, until the cakes have risen, feel just firm to the touch and are golden brown. Turn out and cool on a wire rack.

6 When the cakes are cool, sandwich them with the jam and whipped cream or fromage frais. Dust the top of the cake with sifted confectioners' sugar and serve cut into slices. Store the cake in the refrigerator in an airtight container or wrapped in foil.

Fruit, Nut and Seed Tea Bread

Cut into slices and spread with a little spread, jam or honey, this tea bread makes an ideal breakfast bread.

INGREDIENTS

Makes one 2-pound loaf

⅔ cup dried dates, chopped
½ cup dried apricots, chopped
1 cup golden raisins
½ cup light brown sugar
2 cups gluten-free pancake and baking mix
1 teaspoon gluten-free baking powder
2 teaspoons apple-pie spice
3 ounces (¾ cup) chopped mixed nuts, such as walnuts and hazelnuts
3 ounces (¾ cup) mixed seeds, such as millet, sunflower and sesame seeds
2 eggs, beaten
⅔ cup low-fat milk

— NUTRITION NOTES —	
Per loaf:	
Calories	3,022
Fat, total	107g
saturated fat	14g
Protein	70.4g
Carbohydrate	470g
sugar, total	294g
Fiber—NSP	20g
Sodium	944mg

1 Preheat the oven to 350°F. Lightly grease a 13 x 4 x 4-inch loaf pan. Place the chopped dates and apricots and raisins in a large mixing bowl and stir in the sugar.

2 Place the baking mix, baking powder, spice, mixed nuts and seeds in a separate bowl and mix well.

3 Stir the eggs and milk into the fruit, then add the flour mixture and beat together until well mixed.

4 Spoon into the prepared pan and level the surface. Bake for about 1 hour, until the tea bread is firm to the touch and lightly browned.

5 Allow to cool in the pan for a few minutes, then turn out onto a wire rack to cool completely. Serve warm or cold, cut into slices, either on its own or spread with low-fat spread and jam. Wrap the tea bread in foil to store.

Gingerbread

INGREDIENTS

Makes one 2-pound loaf
½ cup light brown sugar
6 tablespoons soft margarine
¼ cup golden syrup or light corn syrup
¼ cup molasses
7 tablespoons low-fat milk
1 egg, beaten
1½ cups gluten-free flour
½ cup chickpea (gram) flour
pinch of salt
2 teaspoons ground ginger
1 teaspoon ground cinnamon
1½ teaspoons gluten-free
  baking powder

1 Preheat the oven to 325°F. Lightly grease and line a 13 x 4 x 4-inch loaf pan. Place the sugar, margarine, syrup and molasses in a saucepan and heat gently until melted and blended, stirring occasionally.

2 Remove the pan from the heat, let cool slightly, then mix in the milk and egg.

3 Mix the flours, salt, spices and baking powder in a large bowl.

4 Make a well in the center, pour in the liquid mixture and beat well.

5 Pour the mixture into the prepared pan and bake for 1–1¼ hours, until firm to the touch and lightly browned.

6 Allow to cool in the pan for a few minutes, then turn out onto a wire rack to cool completely. Store it in an airtight container or wrapped in foil.

NUTRITION NOTES

Per loaf:

Calories	2,168
Fat, total	73g
saturated fat	16g
Protein	25g
Carbohydrate	375g
sugar, total	240g
Fiber—NSP	0g
Sodium	1,915mg

VARIATION

Fold 2 ounces finely chopped preserved ginger into the raw cake mixture, if desired. Add 1–2 teaspoons extra ground ginger for a more pronounced flavor.

Chocolate Chip Cookies

INGREDIENTS

Makes 16

6 tablespoons soft margarine
¼ cup light brown sugar
¼ cup sugar
1 egg, beaten
few drops of vanilla extract
¾ cup rice flour
¾ cup gluten-free cornmeal
1 teaspoon gluten-free baking powder
pinch of salt
⅔ cup semisweet chocolate chips, or a
   mixture of milk and white chocolate
   chips

1 Preheat the oven to 375°F. Lightly grease two baking sheets. Place the margarine and sugars in a bowl and cream together until light and fluffy.

2 Beat in the egg and vanilla extract. Fold in the rice flour, cornmeal, baking powder and salt, then fold in the chocolate chips.

3 Place spoonfuls of the mixture on the prepared baking sheets, leaving space for spreading between each one. Bake for 10–15 minutes, until the cookies are lightly browned.

4 Remove the cookies from the oven and let cool for a few minutes, then transfer to a wire rack using a metal spatula and let cool completely before serving. Once cool, store the cookies in an airtight container for up to a week, or pack into plastic bags and freeze.

NUTRITION NOTES	
Per portion:	
Calories	135
Fat, total	6.5g
saturated fat	2.12g
Protein	1.6g
Carbohydrate	18.3g
sugar, total	10.9g
Fiber—NSP	0.37g
Sodium	75mg

Cherry Coconut Munchies

You'll find it hard to stop at just one of these munchies, which make a wonderful morning or afternoon treat. If desired, drizzle 1–2 ounces melted chocolate over the cold munchies and allow to set before serving.

INGREDIENTS

Makes 20

2 egg whites
1 cup confectioners' sugar, sifted
1 cup ground almonds
generous 1 cup dried, unsweetened
   coconut
few drops of almond extract
⅓ cup candied cherries, finely chopped

1 Preheat the oven to 300°F. Line two baking sheets with baking parchment. Place the egg whites in a bowl and beat until stiff.

2 Fold in the confectioners' sugar, then fold in the almonds, coconut and almond extract to form a sticky dough. Fold in the chopped cherries.

NUTRITION NOTES	
Per portion:	
Calories	103
Fat, total	6.7g
saturated fat	3.3g
Protein	1.83g
Carbohydrate	9.3g
sugar, total	9.1g
Fiber—NSP	1.24g
Sodium	10.2mg

3 Place heaping teaspoonfuls of the mixture on the prepared baking sheets. Bake for 25 minutes, until pale golden. Cool on the baking sheets for a few minutes, then transfer to a wire rack until completely cool. Store in an airtight container for up to a week.

VARIATIONS
Use ground hazelnuts in place of the almonds and omit the almond extract.

Country Apple Cake

INGREDIENTS

Makes one 7-inch cake

½ cup (8 tablespoons) soft margarine
½ cup light brown sugar
2 eggs, beaten
1 cup gluten-free pancake and baking
   mix, sifted
½ cup rice flour
1 teaspoon gluten-free baking powder
2 teaspoons apple-pie spice
1 medium cooking apple, peeled, cored
   and chopped
4 ounces (1 cup) raisins
about 4 tablespoons low-fat milk
2 tablespoons flaked almonds
custard or ice cream, to serve
   (optional)

1 Preheat the oven to 325°F. Lightly grease and line a deep 7-inch round removable-bottomed cake pan.

2 Place the margarine and sugar in a bowl and cream together until pale and fluffy. Gradually add the eggs, beating well after each addition. Fold in the baking mix, rice flour, baking powder and spice and mix well.

3 Fold in the chopped apple, raisins and enough milk to make a soft, dropping consistency.

VARIATIONS

Use golden raisins or chopped dried apricots or pears instead of the raisins.

4 Turn the mixture into the prepared pan and level the surface. Sprinkle the flaked almonds over the top. Bake for 1–1¼ hours, until risen, firm to the touch and golden brown.

5 Cool in the pan for about 10 minutes, then turn out onto a wire rack to cool. Cut into slices when cool. Alternatively, serve warm, in slices, with custard or ice cream. Store the cake in an airtight container or wrapped in foil.

--- NUTRITION NOTES ---

Per cake:

Calories	2506
Fat, total	120g
saturated fat	25g
Protein	35g
Carbohydrate	340g
sugar, total	214g
Fiber—NSP	6g
Sodium	1,695mg

INFORMATION FILE

HELPFUL ORGANIZATIONS

American Celiac Society—Dietary Support Coalition
58 Musano Court
West Orange, NJ 07052
Phone: (973) 325-8837
Fax: (973) 669-8808

Celiac Disease Foundation
13251 Ventura Blvd., Suite 1
Studio City, CA 91604
Phone (818) 990-2354
Fax: (818) 990-2379

Gluten Intolerance Group of North America (GIG)
P.O. Box 23053
Seattle, WA 98102-0353
Phone: (206) 325-6980
Fax: (206) 320-1172

MAIL-ORDER COMPANIES SUPPLYING GLUTEN-FREE FOODS

Bob's Red Mill Natural Foods
5209 S.E. International Way
Milwaukie, OR 97222
Phone: (503) 654-3215
Fax: (503) 653-1339

Cybros, Inc.
P.O. Box 851
Waukesha, WI 53187-0851
Phone: (800) 876-2253
Fax: (414) 547-8946

Dietary Specialists, Inc.
P.O. Box 227
Rochester, NY 14601
Phone: (800) 544-0099
Fax: (716) 232-6168

The Gluten Free Pantry, Inc.
P.O. Box 840
Glastonbury, CT 06033
Phone: (800) 291-8386 or (860) 633-3826
Fax: (860) 633-6853

Pamela's
South San Francisco, CA 94080
Phone: (650) 952-4546
Fax: (650) 742-6643

The Really Great Food Co.
P.O. Box 319
Malverne, NY 11565
Phone: (800) 583-5377
Fax: (516) 593-9522

Tad Enterprises
9356 Pleasant Ave.
Tinley Park, IL 60477
Phone: (708) 429-2101
Fax: (708) 429-3954

FURTHER READING

Dobler, Merri L., *Gluten Intolerance* (American Dietetic Association, 1991)
Greer, Rita, *Recipes for Health: Gluten-Free* (Harper San Francisco, 1995)
Hagman, Bette, *The Gluten-free Gourmet Cooks Fast and Healthy* (Henry Holt and Company, Inc., 1996)

GLOSSARY OF BASIC TERMS

Anemia – a shortage or deficiency of red blood cells that leads to lack of calories and shortness of breath.
Celiac – a person suffering from the condition known as celiac disease.
Celiac disease – a condition caused by a sensitivity to gluten.

Dermatitis herpetiformis – a rare skin condition caused by a sensitivity to gluten. It causes an extremely itchy skin rash.
Gluten – a type of protein that is present in wheat and rye.
Gluten-free diet – a strict diet, which excludes all foods that contain gluten, such as wheat and rye, and foods such as barley and oats, which contain similar proteins to gluten.
Jejunal biopsy – a test performed under light sedation, which involves removing a small piece of villi from the lining of the small intestine. Micro-scopic examination reveals whether the celiac condition is present.
Nutrients – essential dietary substances that include calories, protein, fat, fiber, carbohydrates, vitamins and minerals.
Villi – threadlike projections that cover the lining of the small intestine and are responsible for the absorption of food.
Wheat allergy and intolerance – a condition that can cause a wide range of symptoms and is treated by following a strict gluten-free diet that excludes all sources of wheat, wheat protein and wheat starch.

INDEX